RIDERS
of the
WEST

RIDERS
of the
WEST

PORTRAITS FROM INDIAN RODEO

Text by Peter Iverson

Photographs by Linda MacCannell

Foreword by Carolyn O. Buffalo

GREYSTONE BOOKS
DOUGLAS & McINTYRE PUBLISHING GROUP
VANCOUVER/TORONTO

UNIVERSITY OF WASHINGTON PRESS
SEATTLE

Pages ii–iii: Shiprock is a familiar sight in north-western New Mexico. This view is from the much-traveled Highway 666, Summer 1993.

Facing page: A bull rider "tying on" his gloved hand to the resin-treated bull rope. Canada Day, Morley, Alberta, July 1993.

Pages vi–vii: Cowboys use the time before the rodeo to share stories and to relive some rides. A Bar C Bull Riders Classic, Fort Defiance, Arizona, September 1993.

Text copyright © 1999 by Peter Iverson
Photographs copyright © 1999 by Linda MacCannell

99 00 01 02 03   5 4 3 2 1

Greystone Books
A division of Douglas & McIntyre Ltd.
2323 Quebec Street, Suite 201
Vancouver, British Columbia
V5T 4S7

CANADIAN CATALOGUING IN PUBLICATION DATA

Iverson, Peter.
    Riders of the West

    Includes bibliographical references and index.
    ISBN 1-55054-700-3

    1. Rodeos. 2. Rodeos—Pictorial works. 3. Indians of North America—Pictorial works. I. MacCannell, Linda. II. Title.
    E78.W5194 1999   791.8'4'08997   C99-910284-2

Originated by the University of Washington Press and published simultaneously in Canada by Greystone Books, Vancouver.

LIBRARY OF CONGRESS CATALOGUING-IN-PUBLICATION DATA

Iverson, Peter.
    Riders of the West: portraits from Indian rodeo / text by Peter Iverson : photographs by Linda MacCannell.
        p. cm.
    Includes bibliographic references (p.) and index.
    ISBN 0-295-97786-8 (alk. paper)
    1. Indian cowboys—West (U.S.) 2. Rodeos—West (U.S) 3. West (U.S.)—Social life and customs.
    4. Indian cowboys—West (U.S.)—Pictorial works.
    5. Rodeos—West (U.S.)—Pictorial works. 6. West (U.S)—Social life and customs—Pictorial works.
    I. MacCannell, Linda. II. Title.
    E78.W51938   1999
    791.8'4'08997078—dc21   98-55931
                                                    CIP

Cover and text design by Val Speidel
Cover photographs by Linda MacCannell
Maps by Stuart Daniel
Printed and bound in Canada by Friesens

The Canadian publisher gratefully acknowledges the support of the Canada Council for the Arts and the British Columbia Ministry of Tourism, Small Business and Culture. The publisher also acknowledges the financial support of the Government of Canada through the Book Publishing Industry Development Program.

FOR KAAREN

FOR KEITH, DUNCAN, ANDREW, AND DONALD

FOR ALICE

CONTENTS

FOREWORD

I first met Linda MacCannell in the summer of 1993. She was taking photographs at the Buffalo Ranch Rodeo. I approached her and asked her if she would photograph my son, Chance Hall Buffalo, who was then two and a half years old. Her patience and friendliness impressed me. Seeing the photographs of Chance really made me feel proud. Linda used Chance's picture in a poster for an exhibition of her work and this boosted his confidence.

Rodeo has always been a part of my life and the life of my family. My father, the late Howard Buffalo, helped organize the first Indian Rodeo Cowboys Association finals in Hobbema, Alberta. As a teenager I competed in such events as steer riding, goat tying, steer decorating, and barrel racing. Four of my older brothers—Todd, Kirk, Bengy, and Chief (Warren)—taught me how to ride steers. They pulled my rope and gave me last minute instructions and watched me sometimes make awesome rides and sometimes make awesome wipeouts. My sister-in-law, Sandy Buffalo, helped me improve my horsemanship and my barrel racing skills. My mother, Dolly Buffalo, my other older brothers, Gary F. and Cameron, and my older sisters, Linda Wolfe and Judy Buffalo, also assisted me.

This book is about family and instruction. It is also about competition and memorials and the next generation. It was important to me to have the book include these subjects. I've been fortunate enough to qualify on five occasions for the Indian National Finals Rodeo—once in barrel racing, three times in breakaway roping, and once in both events. When I have problems with roping, I turn to Wright Bruised Head. When I have problems with horsemanship and barrel racing, I turn to Sandy Buffalo and Marlene Eddleman-McRae. To be a champion you have to learn from a champion.

That's why I've helped organize rodeo clinics with Canadian champions and world champions as instructors. It's also important to promote junior rodeo to attract the participation of kids as young as four and to keep teenagers involved. When you get into the different areas of rodeo it makes you appreciate how much work goes into organizing these events. For ten years the Samson Recreation Department in Hobbema organized a huge Indian rodeo. It was in my father's name and it attracted Indian cowboys and cowgirls from all over North America. My family then retired the first name for the rodeo and formed the Buffalo Ranch Rodeo. All the members of my family and many volunteers were involved with fund raising, public relations, grounds preparation, and the other duties required to produce a top quality rodeo.

In my family and in other families the next generation of cowboys is carrying on the tradition. There has been a whole herd of sheep riding graduates from the Buffalo Ranch clan. Two of my nephews have reached the Canadian Finals Rodeo in steer riding. Todd Buffalo Jr. won the title in 1994. My son is now seven years old and he has already competed in sheep riding, calf riding, dummy roping, goat tail tying, and barrel racing.

Being a part of a book on Indian rodeo makes me feel very proud of my heritage. It is exciting to see photographs of people I know or of places where I've competed. When you look at the pictures Linda has taken, you know that each one can lead to a great conversation. This book captures the true spirit of Indian rodeo. Many of the people included are making history and they deserve this recognition. A book on Indian rodeo was long overdue. Having the best put it together will make it a success.

Carolyn O. Buffalo
August 1998

ACKNOWLEDGMENTS

PETER IVERSON: It has been an honor to write *Riders of the West*. Participants in and observers of Indian rodeo provided essential instruction and counsel. I cannot name all of the individuals who taught me, but I would like to acknowledge the help furnished by Morgan Baillargeon, Jess and Winnifred Beaver, Myla Vicenti Carpio, Hugh Dempsey, Fred and Edith Gladstone, Candi Zion Helms, Craig Howe, Floyd Many Fingers, Harvey Markowitz, Barney Old Coyote, Mark Trahant, and Thurza Vicenti. My long association with the Navajo Nation is also mirrored here. Clifford Beck, Gabriel Begaye, AnCita Benally, Vincent Craig, Dean Jackson, Jack Jackson, Rex Lee Jim, Bill Kine, B. Kay Manuelito, Richard Mike, Monty Roessel, Luci Tapahonso, Glojean Todacheene, and Harry Walters, in different ways, influenced what I have tried to say. The words of Keith Basso, Margaret Connell-Szasz, Vine Deloria, Jr., Joy Harjo, Fred Hoxie, Teresa Jordan, Klara Kelley and Harris Francis, Margot Liberty, George Moses, Richard Slatta, James Welch, Wayne Wooden and Gavin Ehringer, and countless others have affected my thinking about cowboys, Indians, rodeo, and the West. The work and the presence of my graduate students at Arizona State University have also been important. Colleagues Al Hurtado and Vicki Ruiz and outside evaluators for the presses read the manuscript and offered many significant suggestions. Editors Julidta Tarver of the University of Washington Press and Nancy Flight of Greystone Books have provided invaluable assistance all along the way. Linda MacCannell is a wonderful photographer and a valued friend. I close with an expression of gratitude to my family. My grandparents, Paul and Fronie Schmitt, helped initiate my interest in Indian country. My father, Bill Iverson, first kindled my appreciation of storytelling. My mother, Adelaide Iverson, critiqued yet another draft with her customary candor and insight. She, my brothers, David and Paul, and my aunt and uncle, Alice and Harry Davidson, are vital sources of love and inspiration. My mother-in-law, Vi Gonsoulin (whose grandfather rode the Chisholm Trail), my sister-in-law, Diane Ellis (a former rodeo queen), and my brothers-in-law David Gonsoulin (a former bull rider) and Mark Gonsoulin took a particular interest in this project. I thank them and their spouses for all they have given me. Thanks to Erika, Jens, Scott, Tim, and Laurie, for your love and for your generous lives. And to Kaaren, for each day.

LINDA MACCANNELL: Photographs such as these create a bond between the photographer and the subjects. I would like to thank the riders and ropers who shared their images and stories of their families and activities

Wilbur Murphy tries out
Linda's view camera at the
Inter-Tribal Ceremonial
Rodeo, Church Rock,
New Mexico, August 1994.

in rodeo. Two very special people inspired the project and sometimes joined in my travels. They were catalysts. Many of the journeys to rodeos took place throughout the country that my father, Frank A. Mapel, knew well. He shared his love for the region and the people, and the memory of his kindness and respect in dealing with others continues to be an example for all of his family. My cousin Alice Waskow taught me about courage. On some of our long journeys together, we concentrated on the project and forgot her illness. Her lust for life, her enthusiasm for this project, and her company were gifts to me. My husband, Keith MacCannell, and our sons, Duncan, Andrew, and Donald, provided me with encouragement and the freedom to follow this thread. This work began during my graduate studies at the University of Calgary, where Clyde McConnell, Arthur Nishimura, Ann Calvert, Geoffrey Simmins, Laurie Whitley, and James Williams helped me appreciate the beauty of the photograph and explore its power to express ideas. Drew Ann Wake continues to remind me of the importance of the stories surrounding the photographs. L. G. Moses looked at my early pictures and suggested a collaboration with Peter Iverson, who became not only a colleague but a treasured friend. Peter joined me in visiting some of the rodeos portrayed here, and he wove his words around the places and the photographs in ways that honor the individuals as well as my hopes and intentions for this work. Indian rodeo has many who work behind the scenes to organize the events. I am grateful for the assistance provided by Dennis Clah, Shirley Lee, Winnifred Beaver, Jess Beaver, and Carolyn Buffalo. Over the years, the cowboys and cowgirls who inspired this work have been patient and generous. I hope that the photographs and text in this book inspire many stories and reminiscences around kitchen tables throughout rodeo country.

Facing page: A saddle bronc rider holds on for the full eight seconds at the Kainai Fair and Rodeo, Standoff, Alberta, July 1993.

Acknowledgments

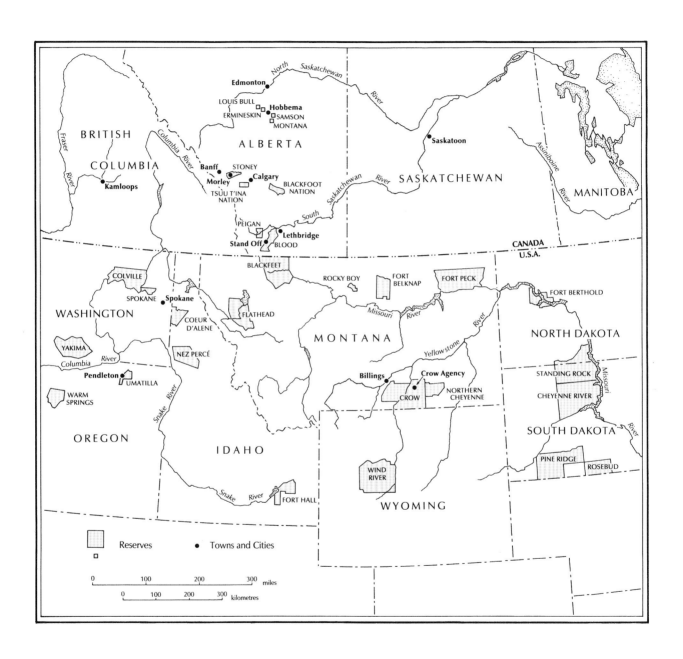

Edmonton

North Saskatchewan River

LOUIS BULL
ERMINESKIN
Hobbema
SAMSON
MONTANA

Saskatoon

BRITISH
COLUMBIA

Fraser River

Columbia River

ALBERTA

SASKATCHEWAN

Assiniboine River

MANITOBA

Banff
STONEY
Morley
Calgary
Kamloops
TSÚU T'INA
NATION
BLACKFOOT
NATION

Saskatchewan River

South Saskatchewan River

PEIGAN

Stand Off
Lethbridge
BLOOD

CANADA
U.S.A.

BLACKFEET

COLVILLE

SPOKANE
Spokane

ROCKY BOY
FORT
BELKNAP
FORT PECK

FORT BERTHOLD

WASHINGTON

COEUR
D'ALENE

FLATHEAD

Missouri River

NORTH DAKOTA

YAKIMA

NEZ PERCÉ

Columbia River

MONTANA

Yellowstone River

STANDING ROCK

Pendleton
UMATILLA

Billings
Crow Agency

CROW
NORTHERN
CHEYENNE

CHEYENNE RIVER

Missouri River

WARM
SPRINGS

OREGON

Snake River

IDAHO

SOUTH DAKOTA

PINE RIDGE
ROSEBUD

WIND
RIVER

Snake River
FORT HALL

WYOMING

Reserves   • Towns and Cities

0   100   200   300   miles

0   100   200   300   kilometres

UTAH

COLORADO

● Dulce

NAVAJO

▲ Shiprock

JICARILLA APACHE

Colorado

River

NAVAJO

Rio Grande

Pecos

HUALAPAI

Coalmine Mesa ●

HOPI

Fort Defiance ●

Crownpoint

Church Rock

□ HUALAPAI

Little

Gallup

Thoreau

Mount Taylor ▲

● **Albuquerque**

River

Colorado

NAVAJO

□ HUALAPAI

Flagstaff ●

River

● **Holbrook**

NAVAJO

A R I Z O N A

NAVAJO

Cibecue ●

FORT APACHE

N E W   M E X I C O

Phoenix ●

Salt   River

SAN CARLOS APACHE

GILA RIVER

Gila

River

River

Gila

MESCALERO APACHE

San Pedro

Santa Cruz

TONONO O'ODHAM

Tucson ●

SAN XAVIER

River

River

Rio

U.S.A.
MEXICO

Grande

U.S.A.
MEXICO

| 0 | 50 | 100 | miles |

| 0 | 50 | 100 | kilometres |

□

▨ Reserves

● Towns and Cities

▲ Mountains

INTRODUCTION

PETER IVERSON: My interest in American Indian history is rooted in family. My grandfather, Paul Schmitt, taught at Haskell Institute in Lawrence, Kansas, and then became principal at the Mount Pleasant Indian School in Michigan. When the Mount Pleasant school closed in the early 1930s, my grandparents moved to the Southwest. During a particularly tumultuous time in Navajo and Hopi life, my grandfather served as principal at Fort Wingate, New Mexico; Keams Canyon, Arizona; and Toadlena, New Mexico. My mother and her sisters often visited my grandparents in these locations. As a child I heard stories and saw photographs from these years; these tales and images inspired a lasting interest in the peoples and places of the region I now call home.

In the spring of 1969, as I neared completion of my M.A. degree in history at the University of Wisconsin, I applied to teach at the newly established Navajo Community College (now Diné College). NCC chose a more seasoned instructor. However, at summer's end, I received a telephone call from a frantic administrator at the college. Classes were about to start and the individual hired to teach history had just backed out. Needing someone, really almost anyone, foolish enough to tackle this assignment at the midnight hour, NCC offered me the job.

I hardly hesitated before accepting the offer. I rented the smallest and oldest U-Haul truck in America and headed toward Many Farms, Arizona. The gas gauge didn't work, and I learned the actual rather than promised fuel economy of this venerable vehicle in Iowa, where at least you are never far from a gas station. Arriving in Many Farms, equally exhausted and excited, I was asked by another administrator if I had come for a job interview. Things soon got better. I played on a basketball team that competed at Teec Nos Pos in the seventh annual Sheep Herders' Classic. I started to explore Canyon de Chelly. I began to make friends. It turned out that some of my grandfather's students, including the master silversmith Kenneth Begay and the outstanding linguist William Morgan, were now colleagues of mine. I may have been labeled a teacher at NCC, but I learned far more than I taught. Living and working in Navajo country permitted me to build, personally and professionally, from the foundation of family stories. Along the way I started to learn about how Native peoples have succeeded in defying the conventional wisdom of a century ago that had pictured them as vanishing tribes, doomed to disappearance.

That story—of survival, of adaptation, of continuity through change—is reflected in all of my work. I have attempted to show how Indian nations have employed a variety of means to transmit values, to build or rebuild communities, to foster pride, to nourish families. I have tried to illustrate that Native peoples have persisted in the face of adversity precisely because they have been willing to adopt new things, and in time, have them become "traditional."

Rodeo is a case in point. Many of my students at NCC were wildly enthusiastic about rodeo. When they read a book such as *When the Legends Die* by Hal Borland, they proved eager to discuss the experiences of bronc rider Thomas Black Bull. Diné faculty, staff, and students competed in rodeo and spoke about its larger significance. In *When Indians Became Cowboys: Native Peoples and Cattle Ranching in the American West*, I included Indian rodeo in the broader story of the decision by Native communities to participate in cattle ranching. Cattle ranching, I argued, allowed Indians a means to enhance tribal identity and bolster self-esteem. It afforded them the opportunity to honor traditional values, including demonstrating generosity to others and teaching responsibility to their children. It gave additional meaning and significance to the land. It furnished an avenue for both competence and competition; Indians wished to show that they could do things just as well as, or better than, their non-Indian neighbors. In much the same way, I suggested, Indian rodeo encompassed such priorities.

This book has permitted a much more complete presentation of this subject. Informed by observations and conversations over many years as well as by archival research and by a careful reading of the literature, my essays reflect a long-term interest in Indian rodeo. But, I hasten to add, the foundation of *Riders of the West* is the extraordinary work of Linda MacCannell. During the summer of 1994 Linda enrolled in a course taught by L. George Moses at the Buffalo Bill Historical Center in Cody, Wyoming. She showed George some of her photographs. George knew of my interest in Indian rodeo, and so he encouraged Linda and me to meet that fall at the Western History Association conference in Albuquerque. After that pleasant initial conversation, she and I began to consider the possibility of collaborating on the project that eventually became this book.

We wish to emphasize that *Riders of the West* is not a documentary or a comprehensive history. We bring to this topic a mutual respect for the people involved in this activity and an admiration for their dedication and skill. In the essays I suggest that the history of Indian rodeo reveals more than a little about the larger story of Native adaptation and cul-

tural continuity, that rodeo has helped reinforce the importance of place, of family, and of competition and achievement, and that rodeo has become a significant Indian tradition. Participants in Indian rodeo have provided a legacy for the generation who will come of age in the twenty-first century.

LINDA MACCANNELL: My most vivid memories are tied to photographs. With a photograph, you can conjure up the smell of a turkey in the oven, the taste of a Navajo taco washed down with a giant iced tea, the temperature of the air, the direction of the wind and sun, and, of course, the conversations.

Peter Iverson and I share a fascination with and affinity for the American Southwest. We both have lived there for extended periods but never concurrently. About the time he was moving to Many Farms, Arizona, to teach at the Navajo Community College, I was preparing to leave New Mexico for another Southwest, the Canadian Southwest, and the province of Alberta.

After finishing university, I took my first trip north to Calgary to work for a year in a research lab at the new medical school. The year stretched to accommodate the cultivation of new roots in Alberta. My husband, Keith, and I were anxious, however, to nourish the old roots by an annual migration between the two hubs that defined our family's orbit: Calgary and the American Southwest.

Those old roots are deep. I was born in Gallup, New Mexico, part of the third generation of my mother's and father's families that had lived in New Mexico. My mother's parents grew up in the area around Silver City, New Mexico, where her father later managed the Chino Mine.

Although I was raised in Albuquerque, I did not feel much removed from the time when lawmen on horseback pursued outlaws through the sagebrush. That era was part of my grandfather's past, and through his stories the West of cowboys became part of my childhood. One story told about my grandfather had all of the elements of a matinee western. It included the theft of the mine payroll, my grandfather (on a white horse) chasing a gang of bad guys (on dark horses), an ambush in a canyon, a rifle broken over a rock, and a promise given and kept. When I stood in my grandfather's rambling adobe and stared at the Colt .45, hung in a holster on the headboard of his bed, art and life intersected.

My father's parents lived in Fort Defiance, Arizona, on the Navajo reservation. Beginning in the early 1900s, my father's father began managing trading posts throughout Navajo country. The stories from my father's childhood were about the trips

he made, the people he met, and the places he visited with my grandfather.

The stories from my grandparents, parents, and others continued to connect me to the history and the places of the Four Corners region. Years later, I would use our family trips to this area to visit some of these places, adding new dimensions to some of the old tales.

My work on Indian rodeo really started by accident. In 1991, I photographed a trading post in Thoreau, New Mexico. The building displayed a huge fiberglass bull on its roof, and the photograph also captured a Navajo man getting into a Trans Am with a "Pro Rodeo" bumper sticker. At that time I did not know rodeo was the fastest growing sport on the Navajo Nation, nor did I know that southern Alberta alone had three separate Indian rodeo cowboy associations. The questions raised by that photograph and my efforts to learn more about Indian rodeo would prompt a series of journeys throughout the Rocky Mountain states and provinces totaling some 20,000 miles and occupy my free moments for the next seven years.

As a graduate student in fine arts at the University of Calgary, I began making portraits of Indian rodeo participants and their families. These portraits have the objective look of documentary photography.

This is photography unplugged. There are no digital enhancements, no soft focus lenses, no traveling stage props. No advance team of photographic assistants scouted the locations. It was just me—with my 85 pounds of photographic gear—pulling into the rodeo grounds, looking forward to an afternoon of rodeo action and some conversations.

Many of the portraits in this book were taken in the dust and confusion behind the chutes. I used a 4 × 5 view camera, which requires a tripod, cumbersome film holders, and a dark cloth. The most important ingredient in these portraits is the co-operation and patience of the persons being photographed. These portraits were all done with the consent, and often at the request, of the subject. The individuals frequently chose the location and brought their own chaps, ropes, horse, friends, or family. They organized themselves in front of the camera while I handled the technical aspects. Because this camera was slow and awkward, the opportunity for conversation always presented itself. The portraits resulting from this collaboration are reminders of those conversations.

Photography provides an opportunity for discovery, contact, and exchange. My family has lived in the West for over a hundred years, and my photographic work is driven by a curiosity and a desire to record something of what I observe and understand from this accumulation of experience. Although the camera has its limitations, it is one of the tools that we have available to continue our stories. It helps us remember and celebrate life's unity, diversity, and complexity.

Overleaf: A saddle bronc ridder at Crow Fair and Rodeo, Crow Agency, Montana, August, 1994.

CHAPTER ONE

History

Before me peaceful.
Behind me peaceful.
Under me peaceful,
Over me peaceful.
All around me peaceful—
Peaceful voice when he neighs.
I am everlasting and peaceful.
I stand for my horse.

—Navajo ceremonial

It begins with horses. To appreciate the origin, evolution, and present status of Indian rodeo, one must understand something about the place of horses in western Native cultures. Historians tell us that Spaniards brought horses and cattle to the Americas. Over the course of centuries Indians acquired these animals and incorporated them into the workings of their communities.

Native stories about the acquisition of horses do not speak of Spain. These accounts say that horses were obtained through a heroic quest by a person or persons from the tribe, that they were received thanks to the generosity of the gods or the holy people. The Blackfeet tell of an orphan boy from their community who made a long and difficult journey. At its culmination he dove into a lake. There a spirit chief helped him retrieve an elk-dog which he brought back to the people. *Sehqem*, or big dog, is the Nez Perce term for horse. The Kiowas say *tsh-achn*, or horse-dog. The Lakotas named the horse *sunka wakan*, or holy dog. The stories from the plateau country contend that the Great Spirit provided horses before the white people came. These horses were faster and stronger than horses brought by those later arrivals, the whites. The Navajos speak of the holy people creating and employing horses long before the Diné obtained them. The Sun and the Moon rode horses. The Sun had horses the colors of the four directions: turquoise (or blue), white shell, black, and yellow. Eventually the holy people presented horses as gifts to the Navajos.

According to one Navajo account, White Bead Woman chanted and then transformed stone fetishes into horses. She gave them to twin boys, instructing them on the proper care of these creations, and they learned about the power, majesty, and beauty of horses. With the right horse, anything was possible:

> The turquoise horse prances with me.
> From where we start the turquoise horse is seen.
> The lightning flashes from the turquoise horse.
> The turquoise horse is terrifying.
> He stands on the upper circle of the rainbow.
> The sunbeam is in his mouth for a bridle.
> He circles around all the people of the earth
> With their goods.
> Today he is on my side
> And I shall win with him.

The horse did not make Indians hunt, trade, or declare war, but such important activities were now easier to pursue. In the distances they could travel, in the territory they could command, Indian nations responded to a growing sense of possibilities.

Raiding offered the means to increase Native horse herds, and before Navajo and Apache men went out on raids they engaged in ceremonies that would give them the power to be fearless, perhaps invisible. If the raider went through the appropriate procedures, he could expect to be invulnerable. The mighty bear symbolized the power of the raider. A Navajo man thus became a big black bear, with moccasins, leggings, and shirt of obsidian. He could not fail.

Since the Great Power had provided all animals, the Crows said, the "Ones Without Fires" had powers not given to humans. "Therefore," a Crow elder stated, "man must obtain spiritual power through animal emissaries and revealers." Joseph Medicine Crow added: "Many Crow medicine men attributed their gift powers to the horse." Such individuals "were blessed with the strength, stamina, speed, and agility of the horse."

Family names in many Indian nations reveal the importance of the horse. Such names could be bestowed by an older relative or elder with that responsibility; they could reflect status or ideals. One's family might have many horses, or one was supposed to grow up to be like the blue or red or white or yellow or black horse in the people's stories. Some family names, such as Riding In, may be found exclusively within one Indian nation. If you meet a

Cory Fox carries on a family tradition in the saddle bronc event, Canada Day Rodeo, Morley, Alberta, July 1993.

History

Michelle Walking Bear
has gained recognition in
several rodeo events,
including breakaway roping.

In 1994 she also served as
Miss Crow Fair. Crow Fair
and Rodeo, Crow Agency,
Montana, August 1994.

Riding In, you assume he or she is Pawnee. A Medicine Horse is likely Crow, a Whirlwind Horse probably Lakota (Sioux). Other names are used more widely. One meets White Horses (or Whitehorses) in Cheyenne, Kiowa, and Navajo country.

Horses symbolized the power and ambition of Native groups like the Apaches, Comanches, Navajos, and Lakotas. At the beginning of the nineteenth century, defeat and incarceration did not seem inevitable. They seemed improbable. On horseback, Indian men performed acts of great skill and courage in hunt and in war. Even when the peoples were confined to the prisons the white people called reservations, horses remained living embodiments of better days and future possibilities.

As the wars drew to an end and the boundaries of Indian communities became more defined and far more restricted, the people faced a dilemma: how to carve out a life on these lands that would permit old values to be honored and realized. Throughout the West in the late nineteenth century, Indians saw their white neighbors engaged in farming and ranching. But most Native men perceived farming as women's work, as the stuff of settled, plodding routine. Moreover, the lands reserved for them were not considered to have much potential for highly productive agriculture.

Ranching, however, seemed far more promising. Although government agents admonished them to become more individualistic and capitalistic, Indians generally remained unconvinced by such counsel. Merrill Gates, an ardent assimilationist of the era, proclaimed that Indians needed to become "intelligently selfish." They should be "touched by the wings of the divine angel of discontent." He declared it time "to get the Indian out of the blanket and into trousers—and trousers with a pocket in them, and a pocket that aches to be filled with dollars!" But Indian men rarely wore trousers with aching pockets. Native peoples did not want to be gentry; they wanted to be generous. Cattle, they soon understood, allowed them to feed both their families and guests. Cattle could be used to pay for a needed ceremony or be given to a young couple when they got married. Learning how to look after cattle could teach young people discipline and responsibility. Cattle ranching would allow Indians to be on horseback again, working with other family and kin to achieve shared goals. Their societies had always valued doing something well. In a period when the whites seemed to be telling them they could do nothing right, maybe cattle ranching could demonstrate their competence and eventually their capacity to do something as well as or better than their white neighbors.

Throughout the North American West, Indians worked as cowboys or ranchers, both on lands that had once been theirs and acreage that remained under Native control or assigned to particular Native groups. Although coastal Indian communities did not generally see the horse as a central dimension of their cultures, most Native groups in the interior West featured the horse as an important element in their daily lives. Indian participation as vaqueros came early in Spanish and Mexican California. Natives also gained familiarity with the ranching business in other parts of New Spain, including what is now southern Arizona. Just as acquisition of the horse by Indian communities moved from south to north on the map of western America, involvement with the cattle industry came much later to Indians who resided in areas such as the northern Plains. But, when the time came, Natives in the Dakotas, Montana, Wyoming, Alberta, and British Columbia proved as eager to become engaged in this pastime.

Within the world of ranching, cowboys performed particular tasks. Wild or untrained horses had to be tamed so that they could be ridden. Then their horses could be taught to accelerate, stop, or turn upon command. Cowboys needed such skills when they herded cattle, separated individual cows or calves for branding or doctoring, or rounded up

The secret to success in
steer wrestling is to put the
steer's right ear in your left
hip pocket. Navajo Nation

Mid-Summer Classic
Rodeo, Crownpoint,
New Mexico, August 1993.

recalcitrant strays, and they used their ropes to throw a loop to catch cattle for branding. Cowboys naturally vied with each other to see who could do something best, although an element of luck or fate also entered into the picture, for riding rough stock was always something of a gamble. From such competition arose the sport we now call rodeo, from the Spanish word *rodear* (a surrounding). But these occasions were initially termed roundups, stampedes, cowboy tournaments, and fiestas. During the late 1800s in Prescott (Arizona), Deer Trail (Colorado), Alpine (Texas), Pecos (Texas), and Montrose (Colorado), cowboys from surrounding and more distant ranches congregated to compete. Individuals from such communities, including persons who knew nothing about horses or cattle, recognized the potential of these events to make money, attract tourists, and publicize the promise of the town.

If rodeo moved from one stage of development to another, the Wild West shows demonstrated the appeal of pageantry and showmanship with a western theme. William F. "Buffalo Bill" Cody pioneered such extravaganzas in the 1880s, taking his entourage to packed houses in London and New York City. Performing before such urban audiences, employees of Cody or other entrepreneurs such as the Miller Brothers (Joseph Carson, Zachary Taylor, and George Lee) of the 101 Ranch in Oklahoma soon learned the importance of flair and drama. Tom Mix and Will Rogers (the son of Cherokee rancher Clem Rogers) numbered among the 101 performers who applied this lesson to advantage in their subsequent careers. Will Rogers hazed for Bill Pickett, the African American cowboy who invented one of rodeo's events—today called steer wrestling but for decades termed bulldogging—by wrestling a steer to the ground. Few cowboys imitated Pickett's signature stunt—biting the lip of the steer as he maneuvered it earthward—but they knew style when they saw it.

These shows had a powerful effect on the American imagination. "Real Indians," George Moses has written, "as the public came to believe, lived in tribes, slept in tipis, wore feather bonnets, rode painted ponies, hunted the buffalo, skirmished with the U.S. Cavalry, and spoke in signs." Even if their participation in reenacted battles and recreated village encampments contributed to popular simplifications, the "show Indians" were far from victims. They used these opportunities in order to travel and to remember. As one Sioux man put it, they gave him "a chance to get back on a horse and act it out again."

By the first years of the 1900s the appeal of rodeo was clearly established. Promoters in up-and-coming communities seized the initiative to create three of the most famous of all rodeos. At Frontier Days in Cheyenne (Wyoming), the Round-Up in Pendleton (Oregon), and the Stampede in Calgary (Alberta), spectators could count on a lot of action and cowboys could count on substantial prize money and lasting fame if they took top honors. From the foundation of those years the core rodeo staples eventually emerged. Timed events included calf roping, team roping, and steer wrestling. Bareback riding, bronc riding, and bull riding formed the "roughstock" events. Steer decorating, steer undecorating, and wild cow milking did not become staple events but could appear on certain occasions.

Women were featured as separate but relatively equal participants in the first Stampede. They competed independent of men in fancy and trick riding and roping, in a relay race, and in bucking horse riding. In subsequent years, they often competed in bronc riding as well as in trick riding and roping. Well-regarded bronc rider Bonnie McCarroll was killed competing in the 1929 Pendleton Round-Up. Subsequent media and public pressure combined with prevailing attitudes among many influential rodeo promoters to limit severely the place of women in professional rodeo. Only through the work of the Girls Rodeo Association did barrel racing appear in most rodeos by the end of the 1940s. Thanks to the efforts of the Girls Rodeo Association, and subsequently the International Rodeo Association, women were able to participate in a wider variety of events.

Each event in rodeo evolved over the course of the twentieth century. The following descriptions are based on the events in their contemporary form. In bareback and saddle bronc riding, the rider has to stay on the horse for eight seconds. His spurs have to be over the break of the shoulders of the horse when the horse's front feet hit the ground on that first jump out of the chutes. In bareback, the rider holds with one hand a leather grip (like a suitcase handle) attached to a rigging, centered behind the horse's shoulders; in saddle bronc, the rider grasps a braided rein. In both events, the other hand must remain free. If that hand touches the horse in bareback or the horse, saddle, or rein in saddle bronc, the rider is disqualified. Judges determine a score based on the rider's performance, but they are evaluating the horse as well, for a rider cannot receive a top score if the horse offers little challenge. When a horse is daydreaming or not bucking much, a rider may be granted a reride. Pickup men help pick up the rider after his effort and escort the horse out of the arena. The horses used in bareback tend to be smaller, but they also tend to be more contrary. In one well-regarded study of rodeo, Wayne

Leon Grant and his daughters participated for many years in Indian rodeo. Now retired, Grant competed in many memorable rodeos, including the Calgary Stampede in the late 1940s. Inter-Tribal Ceremonial Rodeo, Church Rock, New Mexico, August 1993.

S. Wooden and Gavin Ehringer cheerfully suggest that "bareback riding has been compared to operating a jack hammer with one hand, but cowboys say it's not that easy."

Wooden and Ehringer offer no comparable image for bull riding, yet they do remind their readers that bulls outweigh riders as much as ten to one and that, unlike most cowboys, a bull "can easily jump over a five foot fence or lift the back end of a car off the ground." Seated near the bull's shoulders, the rider holds with one hand a braided rope wrapped around the bull. The bull comes roaring out of the chute and the cowboy holds on for dear life, spurring the animal if he can, realizing each time how incredibly long eight seconds can be, maybe uttering a private prayer or a public oath.

Whether or not he hangs on, the rider's immediate future depends on fate and the barrelmen and bullfighters. Barrelmen peek out from a barrel or dash out to distract the bull away from the rider. They are involved in serious business that saves lives and limits injuries. Bullfighters are not clowns, although some may do double duty as entertainers between events. The bullfighter has to be a good athlete and often is a former or current bull rider who can put to immediate use what he has learned about the tendencies of these animals.

Barrel racing, calf roping, steer wrestling, and team roping are the traditional timed events. All demand a greater financial investment from participants. Steer wrestling is an especially popular event. When the steer darts into the arena, he is pursued by two riders. The hazer aids the steer wrestler by being on the opposite side of the steer and keeping it running straight. The steer wrestler rides alongside the steer, grabs him by the horns, drops off his horse onto the steer, and throws it to the ground. On the other hand, he may also realize the impact of the old saying that life is what happens when we are making other plans. The steer doesn't always run straight. The wrestler doesn't always grab the steer's horns; even if he does, the steer does not always consider it a great idea to become better acquainted with the ground.

The fortunes of a barrel racer, steer wrestler, or roper rise or fall depending on the rider's horse. Good horses are rare and they don't come cheap. Only very young boys, girls, and women participate in barrel racing. They ride in a cloverleaf pattern around three barrels placed in the arena and then break for home to the starting point. Riders cut as close as they can to the barrels without tipping them over. If they tip one over, time is added to their total, and almost always this mishap will take them out of the prize money.

Calf roping attracts a lot of competitors and is an event in which older men continue to participate. The rope used is tied to the saddle. The roper and calf emerge from separate chutes. When the roper succeeds in catching up with the calf, he or she must throw a rope over the animal, dismount, run up to the calf, and tie three of its legs together. In breakaway roping, the calf is roped but is permitted to break away, because the roper does not attempt to tie its legs. Breakaway roping more recently has become a staple event for cowgirls. In team roping, ropes are not tied to the saddle. After the header throws his loop over the head and takes two turns, or dallies, around his saddle horn, he goes to the left to avoid a collision with the heeler and to slow down the steer. The heeler then throws his loop, and if all goes well the steer steps into it with its hind feet and is caught. The two ropers quickly maneuver their horses to face one another, with the steer extended between them.

Events also were developed for the younger rodeo participants. In "mutton bustin'," for example, a child is hoisted atop a sheep and the sheep runs into the arena, often promptly depositing the future bronc or bull rider on the ground. Calf riding is a comparable, alternative event. Today, kids who participate in such events may be rewarded with a dollar bill or, lately in Canada, a dollar coin (a loonie). Kids' rodeo has vari-

ous age-graded divisions, often labeled midget, pee-wee, junior, and senior. In the midget girls' and coed division, three- to six-year-old contestants also take up barrel racing, flag racing, and goat tail tying. In the peewee coed division, seven to ten year olds vie against each other in steer riding, breakaway, barrel racing, pole bending, and goat tying. Junior (ages eleven to fourteen) and senior (ages fifteen to eighteen) girls participate in breakaway, barrel racing, pole bending, and goat tying; junior boys participate in steer riding, breakaway, and ribbon roping. Junior and senior boys also compete in bull riding and team roping, and senior boys in calf roping. In some instances, a precocious cowboy or cowgirl may be permitted to participate in the adult division. Some of the best barrel racers, for example, are quite young.

Anglo-American cowboys were the vast majority of contestants in the early days, but as the example of Bill Pickett illustrates, cowboys of color also competed. Indeed, during the first two decades of the new century, two of the most legendary cowboys were Indians. Jackson Sundown (Nez Perce) captured the Pendleton bronc riding title in 1916, the year he celebrated his fiftieth birthday. Some say he was older. Four years earlier, at the inaugural Calgary Stampede, Tom Three Persons (Blood) bested 53 other cowboys to win the bronc riding championship, and he also

Two of the best-known figures in Canadian Native rodeo: the inimitable Lloyd "Too Tall" Bearspaw and Torrin Kaquitts, Canada Day Rodeo, Morley, Alberta, July 1994. In addition to saving bull riders from injury by diverting the bulls, they diverted the crowd in one way or another throughout the afternoon.

Facing page: A bullfighter earns his keep and then some at each rodeo. Here he tries to prevent a bull rider from being trampled at the Morley Rodeo, Alberta, September 1993.

earned instant fame as the first man ever to ride Cyclone, "the Black Terror," after 129 others had failed. At that time, the contestant had to ride until the horse quit bucking. The *Albertan* reporter described the scene:

> He . . . then took prodigious leaps and twisted and corkscrewed his way in a fury of contortions that threatened to tear him in two. The Indian sat in the saddle as if glued to it, with hands up and a challenge to "Cyclone" to do his worst. Again and again the horse stopped, but only for a few seconds, when he renewed the struggle. Again he tried to throw his rider backward, and then, acknowledging he had met his master in the aborigine, he surrendered.

Nor were Sundown and Three Persons alone in their achievements. Sam Bird-in-Ground (Crow) and George Defender (Standing Rock Sioux) both emerged as champions in bronc riding at another major rodeo, the Miles City (Montana) Roundup. Bird-in-Ground won in 1903, Defender in 1914. By the 1920s, Indian cowboys were competing successfully in calf roping as well as riding. Pete Bruised Head Sr. (Blood) won the championship at the Calgary Stampede in calf roping in 1925 and again in 1927.

Nonetheless, such men were exceptional. The size of the entry fees, the distances one had to travel, and the discrimination encountered all discouraged widespread Indian participation in "mainstream" rodeo. Many Native cowboys began to make the transition to roping and away from being so preoccupied with saddle and bareback riding, in part because they believed that non-Indian judges were prejudiced against them. Such an official could give them low scores and thus block them from winning prize money as bronc riders. In calf roping and team roping, one's score essentially rested on one's time. In addition, Jackson Sundown notwithstanding, riding was primarily a younger man's event, whereas roping permitted an older man to remain competitive. Thus Tom Three Persons enjoyed a revitalization of his career when he focused on calf roping. Even though he was nearing forty, he still could compete with Pete Knight and other top white Canadian rodeo cowboys of the day. Based on his experience, Three Persons later advised a younger Blood cowboy, Fred Gladstone, to stick with roping because he would be less likely to be cheated out of his earnings.

Prospective Indian rodeo cowboys before World War II confronted discrimination on other fronts besides rodeo judges. They were not always welcomed by their non-Indian peers or greeted politely by non-Indians who operated hotels, restaurants, gas stations, and other businesses. Big-time rodeos usually featured Indian "villages" or "encampments" as a tourist attraction. Indian participants added a colorful dimension to the accompanying parades, but many Native individuals grew increasingly dissatisfied with this fixed role.

Indian rodeo as a separate but largely parallel pursuit emerged partly because of such problems. Indian cowboys and cowgirls sought to develop rodeos of their own where they would receive a fair shake in judging and also feel more comfortable and welcome. Indian rodeos matured because rodeo served the needs and reflected the aspirations of evolving Native communities in the twentieth century. Some of the most well-established Indian rodeos began as adjuncts to the tribal agricultural fairs initiated by federal agents determined to demonstrate the farming potential of reservations. Such occasions became opportunities for general celebration of community even under the adverse circumstances of the early twentieth century. Indians perceived horse races and rodeo events as more engaging forms of competition than producing larger squash than their neighbors. At Crow Fair and elsewhere, activities soon centered on horses rather than horticulture.

Crow Fair began in southeastern Montana in 1904.

By the second decade of the twentieth century rodeo had become a part of the event. Labeled by the Crows as the first all-Indian rodeo, Crow Fair evolved into one of the largest and most prestigious of Native rodeos. Indian communities also took advantage of the July 4th national holiday as an occasion when ceremonial dances might be permitted instead of prohibited and a few rodeo events might occur. During the first week of July in 1897, for example, the Rosebud reservation in South Dakota hosted a six-day extravaganza featuring rodeo events, horse races, and sprints and longer running events for men. For good measure, the six thousand spectators also heard a reading of the Declaration of Independence and a concert by the Rosebud Cornet Band, witnessed the Corn and White Buffalo dances, watched a parade, and observed a sham reenactment of the battle at the Little Big Horn (with the Indian police and "mixed bloods" drawing the somewhat less desirable roles of Custer and his colleagues).

Although some of these highlights predictably disappeared through the years, horse races remained a feature of many Indian rodeos, and a parade became almost obligatory. Powwows and carnivals also accompanied Native rodeos as the century progressed. When the Tohono O'odham Fair and Rodeo commenced in southern Arizona in the late

A barrel racer clears the first
barrel in the Tsuu T'ina
Nation Rodeo in Alberta,
July 1993.

1930s, for example, calf roping, steer wrestling, steer riding, and horse racing were featured along with a carnival, a dance orchestra, two football games, and in the words of the era, a motion picture show. This pattern paralleled rodeos elsewhere in western North America, where carnivals, dances, and other attractions accompanied competition in the arena.

Native rodeos thus formed a central dimension in a more general celebration of community, in a gathering that brought people together on an annual basis. They became ritual occasions, when people who had moved away returned to visit with family and old friends. They furnished a time when past rodeo champions mingled with present champions and aspiring stars of the future. They provided a moment when a community merged memory with prospect, combined history with a statement of present well-being.

The early rodeos were worth a journey, in part for the adventure. Bronco Martinez recalled being entered by his uncle in one of the Navajo Fair rodeos of long ago: "He says, 'It's way over there in Arizona—it's about a two day drive.'" After he returned from Window Rock, his uncle "was all excited. He said, 'Here, here's your receipt. . . .' He says, 'You don't win a silver dollar, you win a saddle. . . . Let's go, let's go.' So we went over there. . . . It was the first time I'd ever seen a Brahma bull. It was the biggest thing I'd ever seen in my life. And boy, I had a hard time swallowing. My heart, it was about to jump out. . . . I lasted, you know, about two or three spins. . . . Well, we didn't win that saddle."

Thus rodeos offered an opportunity for stories, anecdotes, lessons, exaggerations, and, now and then, what some have been rude enough to label as lies. If these renditions were occasionally at variance with the truth, they still served a larger purpose. They might illustrate the ability to beat the odds, to triumph when victory appeared impossible or bounce back in the face of disappointment. They presented yet another chance for one of the most appreciated qualities a Native person could possess: the ability to tell a good story. The stories inevitably revealed another highly valued quality: a sense of humor. Non-Indians rarely seemed to recognize the importance of humor in Indian societies, but perhaps that was just as well. Many of the tales included a white man to whom something embarrassing happened. "Do you remember when that congressman came to our rodeo? He made all these promises. And the people cheered. They kept shouting, 'Hoya, hoya!' that man finished his speech. He was happy about those cheers. He thought he was a hero. And then someone said, 'Watch where you walk when you leave through the arena. Don't step in the hoya.' "

The smaller the rodeo, the less likely its organizers had to worry about who stepped where. But the organizers and the competitors had concerns, regardless of locale. Judging standards varied widely. Scheduling often seemed uncertain, at best. The stock provided by the contractor for some rodeos was unpredictable in availability as well as quality. A competitor who dominated rodeo competition in one region wanted to compete with his or her peers in other places. Although Indian participants understood that Native rodeos were not in any immediate position to supply the prize money available at Cheyenne or Pendleton or Calgary, they wanted rodeos comparable in terms of organization and professionalism. They also wished to develop a means through which achievement on a regional, national, or international scale could be measured.

Comparable pressures throughout the world of North American rodeo eventually prompted the formation of the Rodeo Association of America and the organization that ultimately supplanted it, the Professional Rodeo Cowboys Association (PRCA), to employ the final version of the organization's name. This association tried to achieve a number of interrelated goals, including the means by which a true

world champion could be designated rather than various rodeos declaring their winner the world champion. By 1955, the organization had matured to a point where its standings, based on points earned at individual rodeos, could be used to determine the top cowboys in each event. Those top cowboys then began to compete against each other in a new National Finals Rodeo, through which a world champion could be recognized.

Indian cowboys and cowgirls pushed for similar measures in the world of Native rodeo. Dean Jackson, Jack Jackson, and Roy Spencer were among those who founded in 1957 the All Indian Rodeo Cowboys Association, the first formal Indian professional rodeo association. The AIRCA (later the All Indian Professional Rodeo Cowboys Association) grew to be the largest of the regional associations, claiming over 600 members in the mid-1990s. The creation of regional organizations reflected local pride and area involvement, and also afforded the chance to improve judging and livestock and reduce scheduling conflicts. The associations sponsored judging and rodeo schools in order to develop better judges and more skilled competitors. They worked with stock contractors to achieve a better quality of broncs and bulls, and with rodeo sponsors to establish a more consistent and predictable schedule of

Dennis Tah enjoys a quiet moment before taking part in the A Bar C Bull Riders Classic, Fort Defiance, Arizona, September 1993.

rodeos. As a good number of these associations evolved, their leaders began efforts to create an Indian national finals through which Native champions could be crowned.

These leaders were often people who had competed at the big-time rodeos and earned considerable recognition. They appreciated the need for standardization and professionalism and devoted much energy and imagination to developing their associations. As Fred Gladstone expressed it, "There were very few Indian cowboys going down the road." In other words, Indian rodeo associations promoted quality but also offered a place for Native cowboys and cowgirls to compete apart from the international professional rodeo circuit. On that circuit, the small number of Indian cowboys either had to haul their families along with their horses and their equipment or had to leave their families behind for weeks or months. In addition, expenses continued to skyrocket and Native riders believed they were, in Gladstone's words, "getting jobbed." Indian rodeos thus yielded results that were important financially, but also culturally. They were often held in conjunction with powwows and thus brought sizable numbers of Native participants and spectators together. Regardless of the common view that only white folks could be cowboys, being a cowboy now seemed to be a good way to remain an Indian.

Native men became presidents and vice presidents of the different regional associations; women generally assumed the less publicized but important responsibilities of secretary or secretary-treasurer. This individual kept the books, accepted entry fees, and responded to a steady stream of telephone calls concerning upcoming rodeos. One is reminded of a phrase uttered by an Indian woman—that "men are the jawbones of our communities but women are the backbones." The women who serve as secretaries frequently come from ranching and rodeo families, and have often competed as barrel racers. If they are married, their husbands and children are likely to be involved in rodeo. They are literally what keeps the associations together.

By the mid-1990s, five regional associations had been instituted in Canada and nine in the United States: the Indian Professional Rodeo Association (Alberta), the Indian Rodeo Cowboys Association (southern Alberta), the Western States Indian Rodeo Association (Washington and Oregon), the United Indian Rodeo Association (Montana), the Rocky Mountain Indian Rodeo Association (Wyoming and Idaho), the All Indian Rodeo Cowboy Association, the Southwest Indian Rodeo Association, the Navajo Nation Rodeo Cowboy Association, the Great Plains

History

21

Page 21: Stetching is also a necessary part of preparation. Uranium Miners' Memorial Rodeo, Shiprock, New Mexico, August 1994.

Above: Team roping proved to be a popular event in the Father's Day Rodeo in Morley, Alberta, June 1996.

Indian Rodeo Association (North and South Dakota), the All Indian Rodeo Association of Oklahoma (also including Kansas and Texas), the Western Indian Rodeo and Exhibition Association (British Columbia), the Northern Alberta Native Cowboys Association, the Prairie Indian Rodeo Association (Saskatchewan), and the Eastern Indian Rodeo Association (Florida). Although the Indian Professional Rodeo Association did not send its champions to the international finals, top cowboys and cowgirls from other regional associations advanced to the Indian National Finals Rodeo. Associations with the largest memberships could send not only their champion to the finals but also their runner-up in a particular event.

Gladstone and other organizers had hoped to put on the first INFR in Seattle in 1975, but there had not been enough time. They then met on several occasions in several different places—Rapid City, Albuquerque, Tulsa, and Salt Lake City—to plan for an inaugural rodeo the following year. A two-time Canadian calf roping champion, Gladstone had helped establish and nourish the growth of the Indian Rodeo Cowboys Association and looked after Canadian concerns in the INFR. Although he was a central figure in the creation of the INFR, in characteristic fashion he credits Pete Fredericks for "really getting this off the ground." Fredericks ranched just

south of the Fort Berthold reservation in North Dakota and competed in events at the PRCA National Finals Rodeo in 1961, 1962, and 1964. Jay Harwood, a Blackfeet health care executive who had moved from Montana to Sacramento, California, also provided important early leadership. During the first decade, he served for seven years as president and then three years as general manager. Yakama tribal council representative Melvin Sampson of Wapato, Washington, followed Harwood as president while taking care of his duties as president of the Western States Indian Rodeo Association. Dean Jackson, from the Navajo Nation, served as another key ramrod in the INFR, and Bob Arrington of Sapulpa, Oklahoma, joined the INFR board in 1977 and later served as INFR vice president. A grand-nephew of Will Rogers, INFR general manager Clem McSpadden spurred the event to new heights. McSpadden operated the Bushyhead ranch in Chelsea, Oklahoma. He has been both a state senator and a member of the U.S. House of Representatives. Active in the PRCA, McSpadden is a past president, announcer of the year, and member of its hall of fame.

Through the years the finals have moved from one location to another. In 1976 the Salt Palace in Salt Lake City furnished the first site. In 1981 Tingley Coliseum at the State Fair grounds in Albuquerque,

New Mexico, became the next home for the finals, which remained there for thirteen years. The event drew good crowds, but northern Natives complained that the long trip was not only expensive but proved hard on their horses and thus affected their chances for success in steer wrestling, calf and team roping, and barrel racing. These objections and increasing problems over availability and rates at Tingley forced a move. Mel Sampson expressed his disappointment, saying that although the INFR was not the Balloon Fiesta or the State Fair, it deserved better treatment. Under the circumstances, he and the other members of the Board of Commissioners decided to relocate the finals to the Rushmore Plaza Civic Center in Rapid City, South Dakota. After only two years in Rapid City, changed management and conflicts over scheduling other events prompted the INFR to move in 1996. According to Gladstone, "Saskatoon came in with a big pocketbook and an offer we couldn't refuse." However, after only one year in this Saskatchewan city, the INFR headed south to Reno, Nevada, for the 1997 finals, and in 1998 the INFR moved once again, to Westworld in Scottsdale, Arizona.

The move of the INFR from its long-time home in Albuquerque had displeased more than a few southwestern Native rodeo participants. Dean Jackson had represented the AIPRCA and Navajo interests

generally as a member of the INFR board. He died in 1992, and it would be several years before another Indian representative from the region followed him on to the board. Thus the decision in 1994 to move the finals from Albuquerque to Rapid City caught Navajo competitors by surprise. AIPRCA official Al Yazzie contended that the regional associations had not been notified of the move but had learned about the decision through media reports. By that time, Jack Jackson had become sufficiently disenchanted with the existing system that he attempted to organize the North American Indian World Championship Rodeo in Phoenix. Although the event did not materialize, this effort set the stage for secession by the All Indian Professional Rodeo Cowboys Association in 1996.

Confronted by the reality of Saskatoon—hundreds of miles farther than an already distant Rapid City— the AIPRCA chose to sponsor a separate competition, which it labeled the AIPRCA world championships. Held initially at the Navajo County fairgrounds in Holbrook, Arizona, the event moved in 1997 to a more commodious and attractive site—the Red Rock, New Mexico, State Park rodeo arena—home also to the Inter-Tribal Ceremonial rodeo. Former INFR president Jay Harwood served as one of two announcers. The AIPRCA's prize money was substantial, and with the support of the city of Gallup, area merchants, and various corporate sponsors combined with the participation of a large number of cowboys and cowgirls, its "world championships" did not appear likely to vanish in the immediate future.

On the other hand, one could make too much of this factionalism. Many Indian cowboys and cowgirls participated in the Navajo Nation Rodeo Cowboy Association, the Southwest Indian Rodeo Association, and the AIPRCA and competed in rodeos that could earn points for any or all three. The INFR and AIPRCA championships were not held at the same time, and thus Native competitors could qualify for and compete in both finals. Three Diné cowboys won championships at the 1997 INFR, and three more triumphed in 1998.

While there might be disagreement about structure and representation, that element should not overshadow the contemporary vitality of Indian rodeo. In the late 1990s, thousands of Native cowboys and cowgirls participate enthusiastically in a sport still in its ascendancy. They compete at Coalmine Canyon (Arizona), at Hobbema (Alberta), and at White Swan (Washington). Whether the next INFR is held in Reno (Nevada), Rapid City (South Dakota), or Red Lodge (Montana), Indian riders and ropers will get there, one way or another. They will come from Tahlequah (Oklahoma) and Toadlena (New Mexico); they will hail from as far north as Fort Vermilion (Alberta) and as far south as San Xavier (Arizona). From the smallest local event to the major finals, Native rodeo continues to foster a sense of place, to furnish a vehicle for competition and achievement, and to offer an activity that bolsters families and bridges generations. It has become a tradition. It constitutes a legacy.

Overleaf: A bull rider can gain a particular appreciation for mud. Kainai Fair and Rodeo, Stand Off, Alberta, July 1993.

CHAPTER TWO

Place

The twentieth century did not turn out as anticipated. The Native peoples in the West should have
disappeared. Their landholdings should have evapo-
rated, their cultures reduced to a matter of historical curiosity. The pattern of North American history
seemed to leave little doubt that by the end of the
century Indians would fulfill the destiny predicted
by Edward Curtis in his famous photograph "The
Vanishing Race."

Native communities did not escape unscathed.
The percentage of tribal language speakers declined
markedly, even within the largest and most insular
Indian nations. Thanks to ill-advised U.S. and
Canadian federal policies that sought to divide up
tribal landholdings into individually held parcels,
Native land bases often eroded. They were pock-
marked, then reduced by land allotment. They were
also lost by cession or taken over in the "national
interest" for use as national parks or for other pur-
poses. Alcohol remained a scourge in many areas.
Surrounding non-Indian populations continued to
cling to the stereotypes and prejudices of their
great-grandparents.

However, Curtis was wrong. The Indians are here
to stay. A new permanent exhibit at the Museum of
Indian Arts and Culture in Santa Fe is entitled "Here,
Now and Always." There are more Native persons in

the West than a century ago. Maps of the Indian West of 1899 and 1999 reveal that despite a series of misguided national policies and prevailing national antipathy, Indian nations remain. This is an extraordinary achievement.

Muscogee poet Joy Harjo writes of "a pattern of survival fiercely stated." Rodeo is an integral part of that pattern. It enhances and reinforces what is often termed a sense of place. Rodeo is, in part, a symbol—of family, of determination, of accomplishment. It represents a testimony to cultural continuity within and through change. It reaffirms one's relationship with animals, with the land, and with the sky. Horses and cattle are a central part of that heritage for most western Native nations. The program for the twentieth Indian National Finals Rodeo states that Indians became cowboys because of their "desire to protect natural resources and to live in a rugged outdoor environment and, more importantly, because of their love for their sacred horses." Rodeos may be relatively new, but as photojournalist Monty Roessel (Navajo) observes: "Rodeos provide a link between the symbolism of the horse and the practical use of the horse."

Whether one participates in rodeo directly or indirectly, travel is involved. Some of the journeys are brief. The barrel racer goes from her home to get her horse and proceeds to the arena to practice for a couple of hours. Yet this is a trip she will take day after day, with each repetition reinforcing an intimate sense of this one small territory, where she coaxes and drives herself and her horse to cut precious tenths of a second off her time.

Other journeys are more extended. They take one past familiar landmarks such as the towering pinnacle of Shiprock in New Mexico or the imposing chain of mountains outside Morley in Alberta. Important places, conclude Klara Bonsack Kelley and Harris Francis (Navajo), may be those for which human use is usually incidental: "mountains, hills, rock outcrops, canyons, springs and other bodies of water, natural discoloration on rocks, areas where certain plants grow, mineral deposits, isolated trees, places where rocks produce echoes, air vents in rocks, sand dunes, flat open areas, lightning-struck trees and rocks." They may also be places where human use defines their significance, such as abandoned or current homesites, sweathouses, corrals; or public buildings such as trading posts, missions, schools, tribal or federal office buildings. Most of these places are not found on maps for tourists. However, they all have names. They all have meaning.

Most of these places gain their significance, Kelley and Francis deduce, from their connection to activities that keep daily life going and that are related to

Place

Page 29: Coal Mine Canyon is known by the Navajos as Haahonooji (jagged). The sandstone formations are situated beyond the Coal Mine Mesa rodeo grounds just east of Tuba City, Arizona, May 1993.

Facing page: This float participated in the Canada Day Parade, which began a day of celebration including two rodeo performances and fireworks, Morley, Alberta, July 1997.

A young girl wears an older relative's jingle dress in the Canada Day Parade. Jingle dresses are worn for dance competitions in powwows. Canada Day Rodeo, Morley, Alberta, July 1997.

stories. Becoming knowledgeable about the cultural significance of a particular place allows one to begin a different kind of journey, one toward wisdom, that sustains life and is, in anthropologist Keith Basso's words, "an instrument of survival." Thus when Basso interviews Dudley Patterson, a Western Apache from Cibecue, Arizona, Patterson contends that "Wisdom sits in places." The stories associated with specific sites are invariably teachings designed to promote proper conduct and healthy living.

The stories may be sacred or secular. In either instance they instruct an individual from example and attest to values and priorities. They emphasize the consequences of decisions. They remind the listener that he or she is part of—not apart from—a landscape resonating with cultural vitality and power.

Rodeo is one of the activities in western North American life that provides time and opportunity for memory, for storytelling, for lessons. The innumerable hours spent in pickup trucks or at the arena are not spent alone. A competitor may be accompanied by his or her spouse, parent or parents, older or younger relatives, peers, children. Depending on status and station, these individuals may be speaking or listening. But there are always more stories: to be told and to be heard, to be remembered, to be repeated.

Rodeo and its attendant activities generate stories.

A particular arena will be associated with a particular cowboy or cowgirl and something that happened—perhaps good, perhaps bad, but assuredly memorable—at this place. The place itself is the stuff of memories: the smell of fry bread, the struggle for meter and meaning within a country and western tune, a certain hue of the earth, the tentative light of early morning, the echo of a meadowlark's song.

Indian rodeo frequently takes place in the context of other significant cultural events, including powwows, giveaways, and parades. These events are especially important in their assertion of cultural continuity, of a people's resolve to honor their heritage and remain on the land. Powwows combine a social gathering of Native peoples with a number of different dances (from the open, general participatory round and gourd dances to competitive fancy dances) accompanied by singing and drumming. Rooted in the traditions of the Plains, powwows now take place all over Indian country, but participants wear Plains style attire, including elaborate beadwork, feathered headdresses, and bustles. Giveaways often are held in conjunction with powwows, to honor a rodeo queen, or for a comparable purpose. They demonstrate the generosity of the sponsors and underline the importance of reciprocity and respect among community members. The feasts that follow giveaways reemphasize those values. Parades are also an integral part of tribal fairs and rodeos. Any person fortunate enough to witness the extraordinary procession of Crow Fair, for example, realizes that the color and pageantry, the seemingly unending line of horses and riders displaying all of the beaded finery Crow art and imagination can fashion, mirror a never ceasing proclamation of Crow pride. Despite everything, the parade says, this is still our home. Because of what came before us, the parade announces, we will continue.

To illustrate the relationship of rodeo to the significance of place, I offer the following images drawn from the 1997 season. There are five stops along the way: the Many Fingers Ranch arena and the Morley arena in Alberta; the Jicarilla Apache arena in Dulce, New Mexico; the Navajo County fairgrounds arena in Holbrook, Arizona; and the Eastern Navajo Fair rodeo arena outside Crownpoint, New Mexico. They all testify to the contribution rodeo makes to people's sense of place and the way this tradition succeeds in blending new and old stories.

The Many Fingers Ranch

It is one of those days almost worth the winter. Whether you live in southern Alberta or southern Montana, you cherish the sudden, unexpected sensation of warmth, of having to squint against that newly discovered ally, the sun. An interminable winter melts in your memory and you congratulate yourself on your good judgment in living in this grand country. As North Dakotans like to say, severe weather keeps out the riffraff. We made it through January; we deserve June.

Announcer Greg Smith (Peigan) asks, "How about a nice round of applause for the family members who got this arena together?" The crowd responds, acknowledging the good work of the Many Fingers family. It is the first rodeo at this particular site on the family ranch at the Blood reserve. The rodeo honors the name and memory of Frank Many Fingers. Together with such illustrious Native cowboys as Peter Bruised Head Sr., Steve Fox Jr., Fred Gladstone, Rufus Goodstriker, and his brother, Floyd Many Fingers, Frank Many Fingers helped establish the Lazy-B Rodeo Club, the forerunner of the Indian Rodeo Cowboys Association.

Accompanied by a recording of a Sousa march, the riders of the grand entry enter the arena. In addition to the U.S. and Canadian flags, the IRCA flag and the Many Fingers flag are carried in for all to see. This is a day to honor tradition and to recognize contribution. There will be a free barbecue. Against the back-

The grand entry is a special moment in any rodeo, but perhaps especially at a newly inaugurated one, such as the Many Fingers Lazy-B Memorial Rodeo, near Standoff, Alberta, June 1997.

drop of tipis put up by the Many Fingers and Goodstriker families, men ride into the arena to be acknowledged by their friends, their neighbors, their families. The line constitutes a who's who of Blood reserve rodeo. The day provides a clear and powerful statement about contribution, about history, about memory. This is our land, the line says. This is our country. We have made it ours through our sacrifices and our stories, our work and our dreams.

Spectators are perched in the bleachers, sitting in lawn chairs; umbrellas shield their owners from that welcome but rare commodity, the summer sun. Kids chase after each other, play catch with a Frisbee, stomp on aluminum cans, ride bikes, even try out a somewhat tired looking hula hoop. There are a lot of three to five year olds. Older children wear an eclectic array of T-shirts emblazoned with team names such as the Edmonton Oilers or individual sports stars like Mike Piazza and Dan Marino. One somewhat improbable T-shirt advertises the Maui Surfing School.

Between events, one can count on two staples of rodeo: recorded country and western music and familiar exchanges between the announcer and the rodeo clown. "She had ruby red lips and coal black hair . . ." "What's that you say, Too Tall?" Smith asks the diminutive clown. We're not always sure we want to hear the answer, but we know one is forthcoming.

All through the afternoon, one hears the sound of families. A mother asks her young son, "Are you going to eat it, or not?" He shakes his head. She turns and queries, "Hey, Grandpa, do you want it?" Nearby, a young couple disagree about who should assume a certain domestic responsibility. She insists: "No, it's your turn to change him . . ."

As we prepare to leave, a bit dusty but delighted with the day, we meet an older gentleman whose vehicle is parked next to ours. "Pretty good rodeo," he notes. "Guess I'm going to have to get my car washed."

Canada Day, Morley

Can this be the same province and the same week? The gray sky is increasingly gloomy. The nearby woods of aspen, lodgepole pine, and poplar affirm that the rain may soon turn to snow. Morley is just east of Banff, and the magnificent curtain of the Canadian Rockies offers an impressive backdrop to the arena. Entrants wrap themselves in heavy coats and blankets as they wait their turn. A couple of people huddle on the hillside, watching the rodeo at some distance. They look like they're freezing. I spot one stalwart in his Iron Maiden T-shirt, but most specta-

The announcer is a vital
presence at any rodeo.
Announcer's booth, Many
Fingers Lazy-B Memorial
Rodeo, near Standoff,
Alberta, June 1997.

tors have chosen to wear jackets. The four concession
stands are doing a land office business in French fries
and coffee, but they are not likely to run out of Mr.
Freezees. We're in the north: bannock burgers with
cheese supplement hot dogs and hamburgers.

I talk with two non-Indian women who run one
of the concession booths. They contrast the environment of an Indian rodeo with other rodeos. Native
people, they declare, will show up for a rodeo regardless of the weather. They won't complain—about
the climate or the coffee. The women emphasize the
respect they have noticed for elders. They praise how
everyone looks after the kids. They admit that going
to Indian rodeos has changed how they perceive
Native peoples.

There is no grand entry, given the weather, but
the Nakoda Nation Canada Day Rodeo does not
lack entrants. Ninety-four teams have signed up for
team roping over the four days; fifty-six kids will be
in the steer riding. Such numbers testify to the
widespread appeal of the sport across the generations. Young people here play hockey all winter and
then rodeo all summer; the mutton busters wear
hockey helmets. On a day like today it is hard to
remember which season is which. I remember an
old joke about Wyoming: there are two seasons
here—winter and the Fourth of July.

Our announcer offers us some familiar phrases: "This cowboy has the skills to pay the bills." And "Saskatchewan is a good place to be from," adding, "That's what makes a good cowboy—running away from home." After a bull tosses his rider: "Well, I've got an excuse now for a new hat."

The bulls and the broncs win most of the battles this afternoon, the weather doesn't improve, and we even endure the macarena. But tomorrow is another day. With the Tremblay Brothers performing tonight, even the evening has possibilities.

It's a long way between rodeos and sometimes a long time between rides. A cowboy rests on a couch conveniently situated in the back of a truck at the Many Fingers Lazy-B Memorial Rodeo, near Standoff, Alberta, June 1997.

LITTLE BEAVER, DULCE

We wait for the parade. My wife, Kaaren, and I have come to visit one of my graduate students, Myla Vicenti Carpio, and her mother, Thurza Vicenti. Thurza now lives in Albuquerque and her daughter is a doctoral student in American Indian history at Arizona State University. A family photograph of her father and his brother, Captain and Steven Vicenti, graces my book *When Indians Became Cowboys*. "My dad always wanted to be a cowboy," Thurza remembers.

The parade and rodeo take their name from a comic strip character I recall from my childhood. Little Beaver appeared in Red Ryder, drawn by Fred

Harmon, who lived in the nearby town of Pagosa Springs, Colorado. Harmon came over to Dulce to look for a model for Little Beaver and found him in Ty Vicenti, today a member of the Jicarilla Apache Tribal Council. After World War II, his family helped start the celebration that bears this name.

The theme for this year's parade is "Traditional Drumbeat Echoes in Our Hearts." The parade is dedicated to Eleanor James, who has retired after twenty-eight years as community center director and is past president of the Little Beaver Committee. Parades also furnish a homecoming for people who now live elsewhere: they return, stay with relatives, renew their ties to family, to community, and to the land. Myla and Thurza greet old friends in a sea of black and white umbrellas, cowboy hats, and baseball caps. There seems to be a never-ending number of Velardes, and Vicentis, and Vigils. We watch the procession of floats carrying Miss Jicarilla Apache, Little Miss Jicarilla Apache, Miss Stone Lake Princess, and the high school basketball team. Where voters assemble, politicians follow. Tribal council members and candidates drive by and wave. So, too, do members of the New Mexico legislature. And can that really be former governor Jerry Apodaca?

We drive over to the arena and find places in the old covered stands, marked by blue-gray splintered paint.

We soon discover that the announcer or the clown must have ties to Texas, because we hear that an Oklahoma Winnebago is a 1969 station wagon with a mattress tied on it. When the clown examines a bull rider with his patented reflex tester, he proclaims: "He's from Oklahoma; he doesn't have a heart beat." Kaaren, who grew up north of the Red River, looks skyward. The banter continues. The announcer asks, "Why didn't you get your mother-in-law a birthday present this year?" "She didn't like what I got her last year." "What was that?" "An electric chair."

There is an occasional Jicarilla competitor, but today most of the entrants are Navajo. However, the Jicarilla entrants gain most of the attention and nearly all of the applause. This rodeo continues to carry out the time-honored purpose of reinforcing bonds within this community; it underscores the long-time relationship between the Jicarillas and the livestock business. Hundreds of people congregate in the stands; hundreds more enjoy the carnival next door. The familiar aromas of mutton and fry bread permeate the midsummer afternoon.

AHOOHAI DAYS, HOLBROOK

It is the first day of August, ushered in by the ubiquitous wind of the Colorado Plateau. The Navajo

A blanket doesn't help much on an especially frigid afternoon at the Canada Day Rodeo, Morley, Alberta, July 1997.

Harrison Curley, a Navajo
bareback rider, continues
on the long summer road.
Crow Fair and Rodeo,
Montana, Crow Agency,
August 1994.

County fairgrounds have been here forever. This is a reservation bordertown, an old Santa Fe railway town. When my grandparents lived in Keams Canyon more than sixty years ago, Holbrook represented "the city." Today people from Keams and from White Cone and other Hopi and Navajo communities still make that journey. Holbrook is a meeting ground. This weekend the fairgrounds hosts not only rodeo, but quilting and model railroad exhibits, and there will be some bluegrass, too.

Ahoohai is the Navajo word for rodeo, a word derived from *naa'ahoohai*, or chicken pull, a popular event enjoyed in the old days when people gathered for different games and competitions. They joked, told stories, and placed bets on contestants. The chicken pull involved a live chicken, buried in the sand or dirt with its head sticking out. Tall and thin riders had an inherent advantage over short and fat riders in *naa'ahoohai*. A rider would attempt to go at full speed, reach down, pull out the chicken, and return to the starting point without slowing down— and without losing the chicken. In the absence of a chicken, people used a mostly buried bag filled with dirt. Then the people imagined the bag held a chicken, or better yet, money.

An hour before the rodeo's scheduled start, a few cowboys wander around outside the arena. Three young women sit at a table painted Pepto pink. They wear sweatshirts that say Chicago Bulls, University of Michigan, Mickey Mouse. They talk and giggle. The half-an-octave recorded music ("This ain't hop scotch, this ain't dodge ball . . . these are our hearts we're dealing with now") starts to summon competitors and spectators. Mothers and little kids are among the first to arrive. They watch their family members trudge across the arena to the bucking chutes, carrying their saddles.

Announcer Ed Spencer informs us that "it's a nice cool Friday evening here in happy Holbrook, Arizona." That extraordinary early evening light glimmers on the bluffs beyond the arena, below a slate gray sky. A horizon-to-horizon full rainbow magically appears. One Santa Fe freight train after another lumbers by. Over the course of twenty-four hours more than ninety such trains pass through town.

The crowd is perhaps two-thirds Native, almost entirely Navajo. The announcements are in Navajo and in English. The invocation begins in Navajo and concludes in English with "in Jesus Christ, Amen." The flags of the grand entry divulge the varied sponsorship for AIPRCA rodeos: Bank One, Bud Light, Coca-Cola, Copenhagen, KTNN, Diné Power Authority, Casper Baca Rodeo Company, T&R Feed, Fort McDowell Casino, Navajo Nation.

Above: Hats and umbrellas
yield shade and protection
on a summer day at the
Inter-Tribal Ceremonial
Rodeo, Church Rock,
New Mexico, August 1996.

Facing page: The view
enjoyed by spectators on
the hill adjacent to the
Morley rodeo grounds,
Canada Day Rodeo,
Morley, Alberta, July 1994.

Place

Indian rodeo, like Indian country, interfaces with the world.

Spencer pays tribute to the veterans, with particular praise given to the famed Navajo Codetalkers of World War II. The Diné take immense pride in the achievements of the Codetalkers, Marines who employed the Navajo language to communicate coded messages during crucial battles of the Pacific campaign. In fighting for America, Navajo soldiers also fought to defend a more particular homeland, within the boundaries of their four sacred mountains. We listen to "The Star Spangled Banner," prefaced by a reference to the United States being "the greatest country in the world."

In addition to recorded music, we begin to hear from a Navajo country and western band who will play for tonight's dance, another time-honored tradition. Twenty-five years ago, Richard Mike's band, The Playboys, furnished music for all occasions— from rodeo dances to weddings. They advertised themselves as "A Band of Wild Indians" with "music for the sick, sinners, ailing and the discouraged." Now Mike owns and operates Burger King franchises in Kayenta, Chinle, and Shiprock, and now the Country Outsiders from White Cone hold forth in Holbrook. The people of White Cone also fund the bronc riding event, with tribal council delegate Eula Yazzie donating the event winner's prize and Vincent, Larry, and Patrick Smith furnishing the added money. Alvin and Sherry Yazzie of the same community are two of the sponsors for team roping event winners. Holbrook may be off the reservation, but it is still White Cone's city, with Ahoohai Days their major rodeo. When "marvelous" Marvin Redhorse of White Cone rides Lady Luck in the bareback event, he receives an extra amount of applause. He and others will have enduring memories of this site, which is, as Spencer remarks, "the only rodeo where you get a train every 20 minutes."

EASTERN NAVAJO, CROWNPOINT

The arena is situated between Coyote Canyon and Crownpoint, New Mexico, on the site of the old boarding school farm. Navajos call the area the "checkerboard," because tribal landholdings are interspersed with federal and private parcels. The fair and rodeo bring together people from the eastern Navajo agency. This part of the Navajo Nation has always felt itself a long way from the tribal capital in Window Rock. Its residents have believed that their particular concerns receive little attention from Arizona Navajos, who comprise the clear majority of the overall population. The powwow

Regardless of how many
flavors it offers, the snow
cone stand is a perennial
favorite. Coal Mine
Canyon Stampede Rodeo,
Arizona, May 1993.

Facing page: A different
perspective of the Inter-
Tribal Ceremonial Rodeo,
taken from behind the
chute, August 1996.

Bull riding is always the last
event, and Walt Dale has no
choice but to wait at the
Inter-Tribal Ceremonial
Rodeo, Church Rock,
New Mexico, August 1993.

and rodeo constitute statements of territoriality, in addition to the chance to spend some enjoyable hours with family and friends. Few outsiders attend, for the only significant promotion takes place on Navajo radio station KTNN. Early arrivals hear the powwow announcer remind his few listeners that the event sponsors cannot be responsible for thefts or injuries or layoffs. "Enjoy yourselves," he adds. "Let's get back to gourd dancing."

The distinctive cloud patterns of northern New Mexico promise a possible shield from the early August sun. People start to head toward the concession booths to purchase Coca-Cola or to select one of the fourteen flavors of snow cones being offered by the Crownpoint Youth Athletic Association. As I take notes on the flavors, a young woman walks over and inquires, "Can I help you?" I learned long ago that the correct translation of this query is: "Why are you here?" I explain what I am doing and she sighs with obvious relief: "Oh, good. I thought you might be a food inspector from the Indian Health Service."

Fry bread, mutton stew, and Navajo tacos are also for sale. It's a bit early, but I decide it must be time for lunch. Announcer Ernie Manuelito, a familiar voice on area radio, soon urges others to move in the same direction. "Go get some mutton stew," he counsels. "It's the breakfast of champions."

Navajo veterans are being honored today. I see the distinctive yellow shirts of the Codetalkers. I visit over lunch with one of these elders. Bill Kine says he "grew up with the sheep" in the Thoreau area (that's "thuh-roo" in this part of the country) before enrolling at Fort Wingate about seventy years ago. He joined the Codetalkers and stayed on in the Marines, serving twenty-two years. A young man wearing a Phoenix Suns cap brings us our Navajo tacos. He is from Kayenta, Arizona, and like most people from that community, he is a big basketball fan. We chat about the Suns and the fine high school basketball teams from Monument Valley High School. I mention that I taught years ago at Navajo Community College. "You must have known my wife's grandfather, Yazzie Begay," he says. I smile and nod in recognition.

At 1:15, five Codetalkers enter the arena. Sam Billison, Harry Benally, Jimmie Begaye, Edward Henderson, and Bill Kine carry the flags of the United States, New Mexico, the Navajo Nation, Arizona, and the Codetalkers. The crowd rises and listens to Manuelito's tribute to these men and their achievements. After the men march out of the arena, we put our hats and caps back on, and we begin to turn our attention to the chutes.

I watch the first rider but I am still thinking about those five men. I remember how they carried their flags and how they carried themselves. I realize they represent another chapter in the defense of this place. Crownpoint is near Mount Taylor (Tsoo dzil) and its proximity brings to mind the story of the Navajo leader Barboncito, who argued successfully that the Diné incarcerated at Fort Sumner in 1868 should be able to return to their home country. If we can go home, he said, we will be as happy as the land. When the people made their way out of exile, they eventually saw in the distance Mount Taylor. The old women and men began to cry with joy at that sight, for Tsoo dzil was one of their sacred mountains, marking the southern boundary of where they were supposed to live. Their perseverance and belief had been rewarded. They reclaimed their homeland.

Near Mount Taylor there are lava beds. The land is covered with the black flow of once molten rock. The Navajos say that the lava is really the dried blood from Ye'iitsoh, one of the monsters killed by the hero twins. It is an area replete with reminders of courage and determination and honor. It is an appropriate place for Mr. Billison, Mr. Benally, Mr. Begaye, Mr. Henderson, and Mr. Kine.

Rodeo is a summer sport; Tsoo dzil is the sacred mountain associated with summer. It is, writes Diné poet Luci Tapahonso, a place where "each summer we are reminded of our own strength." And it is the turquoise mountain:

> *Mount Taylor gave us turquoise to honor all men,*
> *thus we wear turquoise to honor our brothers,*
> *we wear turquoise to honor our sons,*
> *we wear turquoise to honor our fathers,*
> *Because of Tsoo dzil, we do this.*

And so, on a summer evening in Crownpoint, I look toward the turquoise mountain. I think about honor. I remember the turquoise horse.

Overleaf: Children swing on a gate during a day paying special attention to family. Father's Day Rodeo, Morley, Alberta, June 1996.

CHAPTER THREE

Family
and
Tradition

"I remember as a child growing up," bull rider Gabriel Begaye said, "I always wanted to be a cowboy because my father was a cowboy. . . . Some families on the [Navajo] reservation have generations who have participated in Indian rodeo." Jack Jackson added, "Some of these kids today, it seems like they were born with their boots on."

As an Indian cowboy or cowgirl, your first recollections of the sport are merged with other primal memories: of parents, relatives, the place where you started to grow up. You cannot remember learning to walk, but you may recall learning to ride. The world of Native rodeo is built on a foundation of family, constructed, generation by generation, on time-honored values. Knowledge. Hard work. Practice. Patience. Determination. Courage. Competition. Achievement.

In doing something well you do more than bring attention to yourself. You honor those with whom you associate. You know that without your family— their sacrifices, their knowledge, their expectations—you would not have won that buckle, that jacket, that trophy saddle. You begin to understand, early on, that you represent something larger than yourself. You are a member of a family, a band or clan, a community, a tribe or nation, a country. When you compete you represent them all. When you succeed, the memory of your triumph can last for, and nourish, generations.

Fred and Edith Gladstone and their son and daughter, Jim Gladstone and Caen Bly, understand such generalizations. Like all Indian families, they have lived a life of adaptation and change. But in their stories one sees a poignant example of identity both constructed and inherited—forged through experience and place, not simply passed down through the genes.

Fred Gladstone's father, James Gladstone, was the first Native person to serve in the Canadian Senate. Born in 1887 in Alberta, not far from Pincher Creek, James Gladstone was of Cree, Scottish, and French descent. His father had worked as an interpreter for the Bureau of Indian Affairs on the Blackfeet reservation in Montana, and after marrying a Cree woman had migrated to a more northern portion of Blackfeet country, the recently established Blood reserve. At age seven, James Gladstone was enrolled in the new St. Paul's Anglican mission residential school.

The mission school has since closed its doors, but not long ago a Canadian film maker used the site for *Where the Spirit Lives*, a stark depiction of Native life in an isolated boarding school setting. For James Gladstone, the school may have proved problematic at times, but he escaped the trauma typical of such institutions. His friends helped him become not only

fluent in Blackfeet but knowledgeable about the history and culture of his adopted home. By the age of ten he had been given a Blackfeet name, Akainaimuk (Many Guns). At sixteen he left the Blood reserve to attend St. Dunstan's Industrial School in Calgary, but he remained determined to return home. The Blood reserve was cattle country and many Indians north and south of the 49th parallel wanted to become cowboys. Gladstone worked as a ranch hand near Fort Macleod and as a stockman on the reserve. His goal remained a place of his own.

After James married Janie Healy (Pokotun or Little Daughter), the matter of residence took on a new urgency. They eventually would have six children, including Frederick William, born in 1918. Then in 1920 an event took place that altered the family fortunes. James Gladstone became a member of the Blood Tribe. As the Canadians put it, he was admitted into treaty. One is reminded of D'Arcy McNickle, also of Cree descent, who gained enrollment early in the twentieth century on the Flathead reservation in northern Montana, home to the Confederated Salish and Kootenai. McNickle went on to become an eloquent spokesman for equity and justice for all Indians. So too would James Gladstone, but that prospect lay in the distant and uncertain future. In 1920 tribal membership meant land. That

Fred Gladstone, champion calf roper and member of the Board of Directors, Indian National Finals Rodeo, Saskatoon, Saskatchewan, November 1996.

Two generations of cow-
boys, Todd Buffalo and
Chance Hall Buffalo, at the
Indian Pro Rodeo
Association Finals in
Morley, Alberta, October
1996.

same year the Gladstones acquired acreage on the reserve, about five miles north of Cardston. They spent the first two winters in a tent. They slowly began to construct a new life, building a small house and raising a small herd of cattle.

Young Fred enjoyed helping his dad. These were days before tractors, and the Gladstones used two outfits of six horses to work the fields, changing the teams at noon. Fred loved to help wrangle the horses, though that meant getting up early. His parents were strict, but fair. "My parents pretty much let me have my own way," he recalled in 1997. After a pause, and with a slight smile, he added: "As long as I was traveling the straight and narrow."

To make sure he traveled that particular path, when he was nine his parents enrolled him at St. Paul's. The nine year old did not wish to go. "I put up quite a scene when I was to report to school," he remembered. "I took all my clothes off and hid them. Dad finally got mad and loaded me up and my clothes, and it was up to me to go to school in my birthday suit or get dressed. Before I got very far, I had my clothes on."

Students at St. Paul's did not sleep late either. Fred milked forty-eight cows before breakfast but also found time to practice riding and roping. He was fascinated with the art of roping and practiced it by the hour—roping everything in sight (including

his mother's hands). When Fred left school at sixteen, he was an accomplished rider, and roper too. He told of how a resident of the Blood reserve, Chris Shade Sr., "had built chutes and rodeo facilities near his place. On Sundays, many of us would have a mini-rodeo at Chris's place. Often there was Ken Tailfeathers, Buster Mills, Harry and Allen Shade, and many others. It was really a lot of fun," he said. "We had horse racing, too."

Blood society had no time for adolescence in the 1930s. Once you finished school you went to work, and you anticipated being married sooner rather than later. Farming and ranching were the main occupations. With the assistance of his father, Fred purchased a Model A Ford one-and-a-half-ton truck and began a small trucking business on the reserve. On the side there was always rodeo. During the late 1930s, he recalled, "Each little hamlet had a rodeo." He loved going to these community gatherings. "It was a lot of fun," and even if they didn't win any prize money, they won "bags of flour, sugar, and potatoes." He laughed.

In 1940, Fred married Edith Reed, a non-Native from Lethbridge, Alberta. Fifty-seven years later, in the summer of 1997, she still accompanies her husband to the arena and sits in the bleachers wearing a red and black Indian National Finals Rodeo jacket. Half a century ago, Fred participated in the rodeo circuit of the northern Plains, competing against other young men. Now, in the late 1990s, he is in "century club" team roping events, where the team ropers' ages have to add up to at least one hundred. Since Fred Gladstone is seventy-eight, he can team up with a younger partner, but he doesn't need to do so. Once a champion, always a champion: Fred does everything right on this sunny afternoon at the Many Fingers Ranch. Only a lapse by his partner prevents his team from being in the money.

In the early 1940s, Fred and Edith followed the rodeo circuit during the summer. "I was really into roping and horse racing," he observed. "I hauled five horses to rodeos." You haul five horses to rodeos if you are either a glutton for punishment or winning enough to make it worth the trouble. It seemed worth the trouble to the Gladstones. Soon they hauled kids as well as horses. June, Jim, and Caen Gladstone saw a lot of Alberta and Montana. The family hit three dozen or so rodeos during the season, perhaps covering 10,000 miles of this northern terrain. By the time the youngest child, Jeff, arrived in the mid-1950s, Fred Gladstone was moving toward the end of this phase of his life. In his best money year, 1950, he won the Canadian calf roping championship and took home seventeen hundred dollars. There just wasn't a lot of money to be garnered in

those days, even if you were the best. In 1948 he also won the Canadian calf roping championship and made less than a thousand dollars. So he had made his way into the cattle business, aided by some help from a nearby farmer-rancher, Jim Blackmore, and credit from the Toronto-Dominion Bank in Cardston. By 1958, when Prime Minister John Diefenbaker tapped James Gladstone to be in the Senate, it was Fred's turn to take over the family's farming and ranching operation. He was now forty years old and immersed in Blood reserve affairs as a member of the Band Council.

He had started to attend a lot of meetings, but as he stated in a 1974 interview: "Well, I guess this is my first love, if there is a rodeo some place and there is a meeting some place, I'll be at the rodeo." He reigned as southern Alberta calf roping champion from 1951 to 1966, defeating all comers and all colors, for the Indian Rodeo Cowboys Association did not emerge until the 1960s. And he had the considerable satisfaction of observing two more Gladstones, Jim and Caen, begin to gain acclaim in rodeo, while June made her own mark in volleyball, eventually becoming a member of the Canadian national team. Caen Gladstone Bly earned the championship in senior barrel racing for the Indian Rodeo Cowboys Association in 1968, 1969, and 1970. Jim Gladstone did

Saddle bronc rider Gordie Lambert, accompanied by his son, Desmond, and his prize saddle. Morley Rodeo, Morley, Alberta, September 1993.

her one better, surpassing even his father's many achievements in rodeo. Fred Gladstone had learned from outstanding ropers of his day; Jim Gladstone had to look no further than across the breakfast table.

In rodeo, a top flight performer today is first inspired by the example of a parent or another close relative. Jim Gladstone traveled with his dad, learned from him, and was helped by him. When asked by an interviewer in 1975, "I suppose you trained him, did you?" Gladstone responded: "I guess I helped a little bit. He did most of the training himself, he had the desire to rope, and I didn't discourage him or anything like that. I helped him by giving him some good horses, so he's always had a pretty good horse underneath him ever since he started. Today he's riding a horse he turned down ten thousand dollars for last fall." Two years after this interview, Jim Gladstone won the world championship in calf roping at the Pro Rodeo Cowboy finals in Oklahoma City. This achievement by a Canadian Native cowboy was unprecedented in the modern era and is remembered still, not simply by family members, but by others who know and love rodeo. Returning home from Calgary in the summer of 1997, I sat next to a pro rodeo cowboy from south Texas, who happened to be a roper. He had just competed at the Stampede and was flying on to his next stop on the tour. I mentioned how much I had enjoyed interviewing the father of a Canadian Indian man who had won the world title in his sport a generation ago. "Oh, yes," he said in response. "That was Jim Gladstone, wasn't it?"

In October 1963 Fred Gladstone might not have bet a loonie on his son's chances for future fame and fortune. He wrote to his parents in Ottawa, with the usual plea for forgiveness for a lapse in correspondence, followed by musings with which most parents of young men will completely identify, even if they had not been conditioned by milking cows before breakfast: "How are you folks keeping? Fine, I hope. Sorry for being silent for so long. I guess I just wasn't cut out to write letters. have been away rodeoing with Jimmy. I thought we may be able to get along better if we got to know one another a little better, we seem to of got along OK on the road, but as soon as we get home, I just can't seem to get him out of bed and that's when I blow my top. I guess all boys his age like to sleep in the A.M. . . . ."

They do. But as they grow older, especially as they become parents themselves, they gain new appreciation for the role their parents played in their own maturation. Even younger rodeo cowboys and cowgirls frequently articulate the central importance of family. Family is defined in more than one way in

B. R. Amos and his little
brother, Levi Amos, carry
on the tradition as bull-
fighters during the Canada
Day Rodeo in Morley,
Alberta, July 1993.

Bareback rider Melvin
Jones and his son, Chad.
Jones had injured his hand
during his event that
evening. He took off the
ice pack in order to be
photographed. Indian
National Finals Rodeo,
Saskatoon, Saskatchewan,
November 1996.

the world of Native rodeo. Family can mean nuclear family, but given the importance of other relatives in the functioning of Indian societies, it also may encompass aunts and uncles and grandparents. These adults play central roles in the rearing of children. In the absence of a parent or parents, they assume primary responsibility for that duty. In addition, "family" may be applied to people with whom one shares common interests. These may be older competitors who offer technical assistance or personal advice based on their own experience. It is often said in Indian communities that a person who misbehaves acts as though he or she has no relatives. Relatives reassure you when you lose, celebrate with you when you win, and remind you constantly through example and admonition about values and priorities. They tell you that rodeo offers second chances, that tomorrow is indeed another day. They keep you headed in the right direction. When you grow older and emerge as an elder yourself, you remember. And, in turn, you attempt to pass along these lessons to the next generation. It is called reciprocity.

Robbie Whitehair, a Navajo cowgirl from New Mexico, participated in Indian Junior Rodeo. She paid tribute to her grandfather, the well-known rodeo cowboy Bobby Holyan, for sparking her interest: "My grandpa Bobby Holyan used to par-ticipate in rodeos all the time, and he got my whole family to participate in rodeos. We're just another generation of a rodeo family."

You may start at an early age, but you don't have to retire from the sport when you celebrate a particular birthday. Senior rodeo has become very popular in recent years. The Diné Land Senior Rodeo Association has separate divisions for forty years and over and fifty years and over. The fifty and over cowboys compete for laurels in all around, ribbon roping, calf roping, breakaway roping, team roping, and bull riding. They draw the line at steer wrestling, bareback riding, and saddle bronc riding, leaving those to cowboys in their forties. If you were good at twenty, the odds are you will be at fifty. In 1996, Jack Jackson garnered first place in everything except bull riding, where he deferred to Al Charlie. Generations of Jacksons cheered him on.

Whether it is Arizona or Alberta, an Indian cowboy or cowgirl invariably cites family as a key reason for initial interest and for continuing in rodeo. Jess Beaver (Nakoda), now in his early fifties, followed in his father's footsteps. His dad was a bronc rider; he became a steer wrestler. His brother, Dallon, operates a business that provides stock for rodeos. Today Jess Beaver manages the recreation center in Morley, runs the Canada Day Rodeo, and

Marlene Simmons, barrel racer, has just won a spot in the finals. She shares the news with her daughters, Aimie and Chris, at the Crow Fair and Rodeo, Crow Agency, Montana, August 1994.

directs the Indian Pro Rodeo office. He gives credit to Gordon Crowchild, the legendary Tsuu T'ina cowboy, and to the late Bob Gottfriedson, another Indian rodeo cowboy champion from British Columbia. "Those two people really helped me," he said. "They gave me courage and they taught me to overlook my past mistakes. They told me to look ahead because that's what rodeo's all about."

There is great satisfaction in living up to your name, in carrying the mantle of previous generations. Pat Provost of the Peigan Nation knows this gratification. His father, Eddie Provost, and his grandfather, Nat Provost, were well-regarded ranchers and horsemen. In "The Canadian Cowboy" exhibit at the Glenbow Museum in Calgary, one learns Pat Provost's story. He became a rodeo contractor in the 1970s as much by accident as by design. On the spur of the moment, if you will, he bid on the stock contract for a British Columbia rodeo. Provost soon received the good news and the bad news. He had won the contract; now he had to deliver. Together with his friend Butch Little Moustache, he went out to find wild horses, bulls, and cattle. The subsequent rodeo featured so much action that it reduced one old-time rancher to tears. Cane in hand, he hobbled over to congratulate Provost. "I want to shake your hand," he said. "I've relived my youth." Provost was on his way, moving from local rodeos in Pincher Creek, Carmangay, and the Crowsnest Pass area up to the pinnacle of the Calgary Stampede. He reports that somehow his six year old son, Ty, has become interested in horses.

The name itself matters. If you have a particular name, people recall achievements of past generations. They're inclined to think well of you, but you still have to take care of business. And heaven help you if you have a relative perched in the announcer's booth. At the Ahoohai Days in Holbrook in August 1997, bull rider Loren Spencer is instructed by rodeo announcer Ed Spencer, "Don't put the name of Spencer to shame!" Fate dictates that the bull wins this particular go-round, and Spencer is treated to the sound of recorded laughter over the public address system, followed by the cry of "Wipeout!" Bronc rider Mike Murphy of Fort Wingate, New Mexico, "comes from a great rodeo family," Ed Spencer reminds the audience, "and he's keeping up the tradition." Murphy does well; the judges give him a 72. Various Murphys applaud. Ed Spencer knows whereof he speaks. Roy Spencer was an early leader of the AIRCA and a well-known announcer at area rodeos. The bigger the name, the greater the honor, but at times, the greater the burden. Roy Three Persons speaks of wanting to carry on his grandfather's name. "That's why I am doing this today," he affirms. He is, of course, a bronc rider. He perseveres, despite a broken elbow and a variety of other injuries.

When Pete Bruised Head Sr. won the calf roping competition at the Calgary Stampede in 1925 and 1927, he set the family standard. In 1966, he explained why he had succeeded. He didn't let another person train his horse, he kept practicing, he didn't stay up too late, he didn't drink, and he didn't smoke. "Four generations later," writes Caen Bly, "the name Bruised Head still rings a familiar bell in both professional and Indian rodeo arenas." Pete Bruised Head's sons, Chester, Pete, and Joe, their children, and their children's children have all earned acclaim.

The 1989 Indian Rodeo Cowboys Association championships reflected ongoing family accomplishments. Pete Bruised Head, Fred Gladstone, and Jim Gladstone were honored, together with former Indian National Finals Rodeo champions Andrew Hunt, Bill T. Head, Kelvin Fox, Lewis Little Bear, and Wright Bruised Head. Robert Bruised Head captured the year's calf roping honors. His main competitor was Clinton Bruised Head. Matt Bruised Head and Byron Bruised Head were standouts in the saddle bronc event. Just for good measure, Steve Bruised Head and Allen Bruised Head were in steer

wrestling, while Scott Bruised Head competed in the boys' steer riding.

Carole Jackson appreciates this legacy. She became one of the great barrel racers, winning three of the first four Indian National Rodeo Finals in her event. "I started riding in general when I was three or four," she said. "My father was really involved. . . . I'm so grateful to my parents for what they've given me." One cannot choose one's parents, but in Dean and Stephanie Jackson, Carole could not have picked more wisely. One cannot choose one's uncles, but Jack Jackson would be high on any list. Dean Jackson was a major figure in Indian rodeo in North America. Dennis Clah, Gallup Ceremonial Rodeo Chairman in 1993, called him "the father of modern Indian rodeo." A top-notch roper and rider, Jackson helped organize the All Indian Rodeo Cowboys Association, served as its first president, and labored as one of the board members responsible for developing the Indian National Finals Rodeo. When Clah sought his counsel about whether he should help out with the Ceremonial Rodeo, Jackson replied, "Brother, remember. You are not doing this for yourself, but for all the Indian cowboys and cowgirls—both yesterday and tomorrow—who compete at the Ceremonial Rodeo."

Team roping is an event that, literally, encourages family ties. Two brothers often work as a team, and

Bareback rider Larry "The Kid" Daniels began riding at the age of three. Here he looks forward to competing in the Canada Day Rodeo, Morley, Alberta, July 1994.

pairs of brothers from a large family sometimes compete. In the Cree community of Hobbema, for example, Merle, Marvin, Dion, and Carter Yellowbird all participated in team roping. They took on other teams with familiar names: Labelle, Lefthand, Bruised Head, Day Chief, Buffalo, and, upon occasion, Ramone. The nine Ramone brothers grew up in Crownpoint but eventually went their separate ways. Even though they lived in Utah, Idaho, Montana, and New Mexico, they drove hundreds of miles to team up at various rodeos. If you win over $8,000 in a weekend, as four Ramone brothers did at White Swan on Yakama in 1993, the 775-mile drive back to Salt Lake City isn't bad at all. In 1989, Emerson and Benny Ramone won the INFR team roping title; in 1991, Leo and Benson Ramone finished second to another Navajo brother team, Reggie and Lucius Sells, of Chinle, Arizona. The Ramone and Sells brothers are a recent example of siblings combining for this championship; they were preceded by Gary and Sandy Rogers (Yerington, Nevada), Gary and Randy Rogers (Sparks, Nevada), Wayne and Wally Dennison (Tohatchi, New Mexico), Ollie and Mike Benjamin (Morley, Alberta), and Leonard and Leslie Williams (Flagstaff, Arizona).

But not all brothers get along, and not every cowboy is a devoted family man. Modoc cowboy Sonny Jim became a bit of a legend in Navajo country a generation ago. A charismatic guy, he captivated school kids, who liked his looks and style. Several young students even fashioned a volume they labeled the "First Book of Sonny Jim." "Sonny Jim is like a hippie," wrote Bobby Benally and his pals. "He has long hair with an old headband. . . . He has white old cowboy boots with spurs. He is a brave man, he is not afraid of all kinds of bull." That assertion, by all reports, was true. However, years later his daughter, Sonlatsa Jim-James, identified herself in this way: "I am the daughter of Elouise Johnson, full-blooded Navajo, a full-time mother, and constant victim of the U.S. policies on Indian lands. My father, Sonny Jim, is a part-time father and full-time Indian rodeo cowboy."

By contrast, Hobert Pourier was no part-time father. By the time he passed away in 1993, he and his wife, Isabella, claimed not only 11 children, but 75 grandchildren, 128 great-grandchildren, and 24 great-great-grandchildren. Pourier mirrored Dean Jackson in his dedication to the sport of rodeo and in the impact he had on his family. He had come of age during the wrenching era of the 1920s and 1930s—a period that gripped the Dakotas and simply would not let go. Grasshoppers were as big as birds at that time, one of his sons recalled. One way or another,

Pourier met the challenge. He always worked hard to support his family. When he was seventy-six he participated in the finals of the Old Man's Breakaway in the Sioux Nation Rodeo. Reporter Avis Little Eagle noted in his obituary: "Many will remember him as a hard worker, whose strength, fortitude and horseman's skills made him great."

Pourier was blessed with four score years, but Dean Jackson died too young, a victim of cancer. His name now graces the rodeo arena at Window Rock. In 1993, the year following his death, the Gallup Ceremonial Board of Directors honored him and his family by dedicating the year's rodeo to "this man who meant so much to so many." In the following month of September, at the annual gathering called the Navajo Nation Fair, the first annual Dean Jackson Memorial Rodeo took place.

The tradition of memorials reveals an integral dimension of Native rodeo. Throughout Indian country one sees versions of this practice. A family will honor the memory of one who has passed away by sponsoring a particular rodeo, or an event at a rodeo, for one or more years. A manager of a rodeo will use this occasion to honor relatives by praising their past achievements in testimonials printed in the rodeo program. Members of a particular band or community will pay tribute to one of their own or several of their own through their support, both financial and otherwise, of a new or ongoing rodeo.

In 1994, Lawrence Pretty Weasel tackled a not entirely enviable assignment: managing the Crow Fair Rodeo. Regardless of the headaches encountered in organizing and running such a premier event, Pretty Weasel declared in the rodeo program that he was "honored to continue the family tradition of managing the 76th annual Crow Fair Rodeo." His great-grandfathers, after all, had been "instrumental" in its creation, and he had enjoyed a long and successful rodeo career, qualifying on two occasions for the Indian National Finals Rodeo in team roping.

The program for the 1994 Crow Fair Rodeo reflects Pretty Weasel's respect for his family. The cover photograph, taken at the 1976 Crow Fair, is of his late great-grandfather, Paul Williamson, an outstanding bronc rider of the 1930s. The back cover portrays Dexter Williamson Jr., a great-uncle who also excelled in the years before World War II. Another page is devoted "in loving memory of Gregory Pretty Weasel": "an excellent horseman, he enjoyed being around horses, training race horses and breaking horses. He also enjoyed roping." And on an additional page Gary Not Afraid, the uncle of Lawrence Pretty Weasel, is remembered. He also came from a rodeo family: brothers Leo, Cedric, and Edward Not Afraid had been first-rate bronc riders. Born in 1941, Gary Not Afraid "represented the Crow Indian people by serving as a good will ambassador, as an all around competitor in the sport of rodeo." Not Afraid won the calf roping championship at the first INFR. The tribute in the rodeo program reflects upon his many accomplishments in rodeo and concludes: "Today, Gary Paul Not Afraid is not with us but gone beyond the Great Shining Mountains where the pasture is green, luscious, and the river flows forever."

The memorials thus provide a culturally appropriate means to express grief and to bestow honor. Life is as fragile in Indian country as elsewhere. Rodeo announcer Randy Gaudry says that travel to rodeos is more dangerous than being in the rodeo. When Levi Black Water Sr. died in a tragic accident in 1991, the newspapers spoke of his considerable achievements in the world of rodeo and his service to the Blood reserve as a councilor. "Great men accomplish great things," they said at his service. He was lauded for teaching his children "how to maintain the proper care and attention to their horses" and for instilling "a competitive spirit" in them. His son, Levi Jr., spoke about his father's work ethic and the priority he placed upon family.

The Levi Black Water Sr. memorial rodeo in the following year gave his family and his community another opportunity to honor his memory. The first rodeo was a great success and, it was observed, "it was only fitting that his son Levi Jr. won the first Memorial." Before the second memorial rodeo in 1993, a newspaper story proclaimed, "The saga of Levi Black Water Sr. will continue to live on in the hearts of those he touched as he watches over his loved ones from the winners circle in cowboy heaven." The idea of a cowboy heaven is pervasive in Indian country and knows no tribal or denominational boundaries. When Hobert Pourier of Porcupine, South Dakota, passed away, Larry Pourier said, "I'll tell you one thing, if there's a horse race in heaven, I'll bet the Lord just made Grandpa the Ranch Foreman."

If a rodeo participant or members of his or her family happen to be Christian, there may be a reference to Jesus in the memorial. For example, a Kananaskis Rodeo program included the following tribute to Trevor "Tuffy" Holloway:

A final nod for the chute gate
for an endless ride
but not upon a raging bull
but with the Lord by his side.
For within my heart

Trevor "Tuffy" Holloway,
bull rider, immediately after
a difficult eight-second ride
at the Morley Rodeo,
Alberta, September 1993.
Through memorials,
Holloway and other
competitors are honored
and remembered.

I made the perfect score.
With the Lord Jesus Christ as my judge
I will live forever more.

Ultimately it does not seem to matter whether a person who has passed away is a Christian, a traditionalist, or a member of the Native American Church. Dean Jackson was hardly alone in finding meaning in all three of these forms of religious expression. The cowboy prayer, recited customarily in the beginning moments of a rodeo, speaks of "the Creator" generally, rather than God the Father. This prayer forms the basis for a variety of memorial tributes. For team roper Dale David "Tazz" Big Plume (Tsuu T'ina), then, whose rodeo partner, Bob Noel, had already passed away, the memorial tribute would read something like: "His rodeo partner will meet him at the Creator's Rodeo Office and together they will continue their trail of peace in that circuit, with their dues paid in full." The notion about dues comes directly from the cowboy prayer. This version appeared in the Kainai Fair and Rodeo program in 1993:

> Heavenly Father, we pause mindful of the many blessings you have bestowed upon us. We ask that you be with us at this rodeo and we pray that you will guide us in the arena of life. We don't ask for special favors; we don't ask to draw a chute fighting horse or to never break a barrier. Nor do we ask for all daylight runs or not to draw a steer that won't lay. Help us, Lord, to live our lives in such a manner that when we make the last inevitable ride to the country up there, where the grass grows green and stirrup-high, and the water runs cool, clear, and deep, that you, as our last Judge, will tell us that our entry fees have been paid.

This sense of "the country up there" is phrased in more alpine terms by those who live within sight of the mountains. If you hail from country where wind prevails, then you refer to wind. In this special place there will be all the major elements of life on earth, including music, horses, and the wind. Levi Black Water loved the music of Elvis Presley. Black Water's favorite horse was Buck, a buckskin gelding. Managing editor of the *Kainai News*, Tom Russell, thus wrote: "Somewhere up there in cowboy heaven sits the king of rock 'n roll with a cowboy hat on and the king of rodeo with a guitar in his hands, singing songs and reliving the legacies they left behind." When Buck died, Russell observed: "One of the Blood reserve's greatest athletes and teachers has passed on into that rodeo in the sky. . . . Buck, a 24 year old buckskin gelding . . . was buried on the ranch he was born on and his spirit is now with Levi Sr.—running free in the wind and in the hearts of his family."

I think about the hearts of families, the long memories, the lasting respect that are a central part of Indian rodeo. Nowhere, I conclude, could it be more fully mirrored than at the Many Fingers Rodeo. On that glorious afternoon in the summer of 1997, I watch Edith Gladstone and Pauline Gladstone Dempsey and Hugh Dempsey sitting together in the stands, exchanging stories, smiling. I meet Floyd Many Fingers and other individuals who have invested so much of themselves in this evolving, ongoing tradition.

I remember an essay by Joy Harjo, "The Place of Origins." And though she evokes another place and another time, her words speak to the meaning of this secular gathering on this land. "Stories here," she declares, "are as thick as insects singing. We were part of the ongoing story of the people." The new rodeo and the new rodeo arena constructed by the Many Fingers family yield a living tribute to those who have gone before. Fifty-nine years before, Frank Many Fingers carried his family's flag when he journeyed with other Native cowboys to Australia. Today Buck Many Fingers carries the same flag into this new arena. Ed Little Bear was a highly successful rodeo cowboy. Today his grandson rides. To no one's surprise, a Bruised Head, Robert, leads the calf roping and steer wrestling. Announcer Greg Smith makes explicit the connection between generations. When Steve Fox's grandson Stephen appears, Smith declares: "Here is Stephen Fox carrying on that tradition."

The crowd particularly appreciates the efforts of the "century club" team ropers: Pete and Joe Bruised Head, Fred Gladstone and Lawrence Crawler, Gordon McDougal and Sidney Starlight, Floyd Many Fingers and James Plain Eagle, and various other combinations of seniors. Announcer Smith introduces one old-timer after another: "Mr. Raymond Young Pine, wave your hat to the crowd. Good to have you here, Ray." Smith praises the Gladstones—Fred and Edith and Fred's brother, Horace. They are the pioneers of rodeo in Indian country, he says.

They are pioneers, cowboys, and Indians. They are family.

Overleaf: Riding a twister! A bull rider stays on for the full eight seconds during the Inter-Tribal Ceremonial Rodeo, Church Rock, New Mexico, August 1993.

CHAPTER FOUR

Competition and Achievement

Up and down he bucks so bad
For this old bull is really mad
He bellers and snorts and throws his head back
I'm sure glad I left a little slack
For many a cowboy I've seen jerked down
they'd have really been hurt if not for the clown
Well, he jumps and kicks and throws me off
It's a damn good thing I'm awful tough
He's coming now, I've got to get up and run
For if he ever hooks me I know I'm done
His eyes are wide, his horns are wider
Why'd I ever become a damn Bull Rider?

—ANONYMOUS DOGGEREL PUBLISHED IN
DINÉ BAA-HANI

This is rodeo's most dangerous event, and can cause serious injury or even death. When you learn that someone rides bulls—or ever rode bulls—that bit of knowledge gives you extra insight about the person. Or perhaps it just confirms your suspicions that this individual is . . . well . . . some day I'll have to introduce you to my brother-in-law, a former bull rider.

Younger cowboys, not yet old enough to be allowed to ride bulls, enter steer riding and dream of when they can take on the quite literally larger challenge. Ben Hart from the Three Affiliated Tribes in North Dakota competes at Crow Fair in 1994 and looks forward to the day when he can be a part of this main event. But not all those who dream are cowboys. Glenna Goodstoney (Nakoda) believes she will be up to that ultimate challenge. "My dream is to ride bulls," she says. Today she must still ride steers. Looking older than her years, she sits in the bleachers, smokes a cigarette, and awaits her turn.

Although not equal in seasons with older participants, they are already equal in their desire to compete and achieve—objectives deeply rooted in Indian societies. These objections precede the arrival of the white people; they extend as far back as the ancient stories that still convey the teachings of Native communities. The hero twin stories of the Navajos are but one example of tales that again and again introduce a person (or persons) who must undergo some kind of journey, confront risks and dangers, overcome such adversity through self-assertion and self-discipline, and return in hard-earned triumph. Traditional stories tell of races to be run and games to be won. They reflect the importance of doing something well—of being somebody.

The young women who compete for such titles as Miss Crow Fair or Miss All Indian Rodeo Cowboys Association or Miss Indian Rodeo North America do not have to endure the same degree of physical testing, but the honors they vie for demand many of the same qualities. Those who earn these designations are ambassadors representing a particular event. As such, they must be attractive, speak well, know about the community that sponsors the rodeo, and be able to ride. They help escort steers and calves out of the arena after roping events. For T. J. Maloney, Miss AIRCA for 1992–93, it's all in a day's work. Not surprisingly, then, most are also barrel racers or breakaway ropers. Michelle Walking Bear, Miss Crow Fair of 1994, began to participate in rodeo when she was five and became a competitive barrel racer and breakaway roper and most recently has entered team roping.

A woman in rodeo is at a disadvantage in competing for the all around title at a particular rodeo or over the season for a rodeo association, because she cannot participate in as many events as a man. But if she dominates her events, such accomplishments are possible, even though the odds are quite formidable. Janelle Manygoats captured the 1997 AIPRCA all-around title, just as Carole Jackson did during another memorable rodeo season. As Jackson neared her goal, she noticed that some of the men "had a lot of mixed feelings" about her success. She observed that the older cowboys she had grown up with were pulling for her: "They were really rootin' for me and some of them, they just didn't say anything; it was just what I could feel as a woman beating them in the all around. . . . It was truly amazing the feeling, you know. . . . I was really honored."

In the different events, individual competitors are always conscious of where they stand. The tribal newspapers publish rankings as the season moves along. The winners at each rodeo gain publicity for their accomplishments. Your point totals add up as time goes on; if you finish near the top, you qualify to compete in the regional finals. As we have noted, as of 1996, the AIRCA finals became an end in itself. But in any of the other twelve regional finals, you compete for the opportunity to represent your association at the Indian National Finals. Win at the national finals and your name becomes part of the pantheon of greats.

Ten year old steer rider
Ben Hart has journeyed
from Fort Berthold, North
Dakota, to compete at the
Crow Fair and Rodeo,
Crow Agency, Montana,
August 1994.

Competition and Achievement

Billie Rose stops briefly for this photograph before hurrying away to round up calves loose in the arena following the calf roping competition. Crow Fair and Rodeo, Crow Agency, Montana, August 1994.

That list of Indian world champions makes for good company. For any longtime fan of Native rodeo, the parade of names conjures up a host of memories of outstanding achievement. In the national finals from 1976 to 1996, cowboys and cowgirls recorded impressive triumphs. One remembers Jim Jacobs of Porcupine, South Dakota, winning the bareback riding championship six times and Howard Hunter of Kyle, South Dakota, capturing four saddle bronc riding titles. One recalls Carole Jackson of Tsaile, Arizona, and Kerri Adams of Stuart, Oklahoma, each gaining three barrel racing championships and John Boyd Jr. of Window Rock, Arizona, taking three titles in calf roping. John Colliflower of Rocky Boy, Montana, and Jacob Antone of Crownpoint, New Mexico, twice took top honors in steer wrestling. Britt Givens of Arapahoe, Wyoming, Dale Bird of Browning, Montana, and Dave Best of Omak, Washington, garnered two championships each in bull riding. In team roping, Dee Keener of Inola, Oklahoma, won four times in a row, twice teaming with Chuck Morgan of Comanche, Oklahoma, and then twice combining with Joel Maker of Tahlequah, Oklahoma. When it came to all around cowboy honors, Jerry Small, of Busby, Montana, won three times and tied for first on a fourth occasion.

Winning at the national finals remains a vivid memory for those few who achieve it. It is a moment to be replayed in one's mind, a well to be drawn from at some future point when unanticipated misfortunes have made you doubt your future. Whatever you may accomplish in the days to come, you will always be recognized for that attainment.

That moment finally arrived for Andrew Hunt in 1986. This third-generation cowboy from the Blood reserve had been an INFR participant for nine years. He had earned an average of ten thousand dollars a year over the past decade. So he had demonstrated he could compete with the best, but he had not realized his ambition of a championship. In the 1986 season he participated in about forty-five Indian and professional rodeos leading up to the finals in Albuquerque. There he did not win an individual title, as had his Blood compatriots Bill T. Head and Lewis Little Bear. But his combined scores in calf roping and steer wrestling proved sufficient to earn him the all around honors. When asked to express his feelings about his win, Hunt replied in the less than loquacious style embraced by many cowboys, whose traditionally taciturn responses suggest they believe they have only been allotted so many words and they are not about to squander a significant portion of them on one occasion. "It feels pretty good," he said.

Saddle bronc champion Lewis Little Bear, by

A barrel racer, Tsuu T'ina
Nation Rodeo, Alberta,
July 1993.

Facing page: Calf roper,
Canada Day Rodeo,
Morley, Alberta, July 1994.

Competition and Achievement

79

Bill T. Head, bronc rider, getting ready to go down the road from the Kainai Fair and Rodeo, Standoff, Alberta, July 1993. He has just won a saddle. Seven years earlier he had emerged victorious in the bareback event in the Indian National Finals Rodeo.

contrast, took out a large advertisement in the *Kainai News.* "Thank You From Lewis Little Bear," it begins. "A very special 'Thank-You' to all you 'well wishers' who supported me both financially and through prayer on my trip to the INFR in Albuquerque, NM. My 'Hats off' to Bill T. Head and Andrew Hunt on their victories and especially to the rest of my fellow IRCA and Blood finalists who competed at the INFR." He thanks "numerous people who have supported me throughout my rodeo career," beginning with his wife, Jackie, and their sons, J. J. and Nolan, and proceeds to thank a host of others, with the names of Levi and Theresa Black Water at the top of the list.

From the era of Tom Three Persons and Jackson Sundown to our own time, Native cowboys and cowgirls have distinguished themselves in professional rodeos. In addition to Jim Gladstone's triumph in 1977, Bud Longbrake (Lakota) won the 1990 PRCA saddle bronc title. Many Native cowboys have excelled at the Calgary Stampede. King Bearspaw, Bill McLean, John Left Hand, and Fred Gladstone all won in wild cow milking, and Jim Wells Sr. and Henry Dodging Horse won in steer decorating, the precursor to steer wrestling. Linda One Spot (Tsuu T'ina) assumed the alias of Linder One Spot so she could compete in the boys' steer riding event in 1952. She finished first.

There is a relatively straight line that runs from the old stories to the present. All along the way, we perceive examples of courage, of testing and proving oneself, of gaining the respect of one's peers. In another time, war required ritual, discipline, and knowledge. The young learned about such matters from the teachings of elders, from observation, and from experience. The people fought not only to demonstrate bravery, but to win.

The stakes are of course not the same in a rodeo arena or on a basketball court or on a cross-country course, but such sports do exemplify modern means of realizing time-honored virtues. In this contemporary competition, then, participants simultaneously represent themselves, their families, their communities, their tribe or nation. When Dave Archambault coached at Little Wound School on Pine Ridge, he said: "I teach our athletes that we can run and play ball for the Lakota Nation; but more specifically, for the Oglala band. We are trying to say to the world we are fine athletes, both men and women. We are the best Native Americans in the world." Archambault added: "We run and play ball for the good that it will bring to our families, community, and our school. It will bring pride to our people. It is the modern way of counting coup. It helps our young want to grow up and do great things, makes them aspire to greatness. Our doing good or being the best helps our people in many ways."

In her study of one northern Plains community, Loretta Fowler observed: "At the same time that Gros Ventres competed among each other for prominence, they competed with other tribes for primacy. In fact, there was a fit between pursuit of individual prominence and the pursuit of primacy." Thus in the major rodeos, spectators and participants compare how well entrants from one Indian nation fare against another. Before the 1996 Tsuu T'ina Indian Cowboy Memorial Rodeo, Kevin Littlelight notes: "We are the smallest tribe in Treaty 7, but we seem to be pretty competitive, given the population we have." The Crow Fair rodeo program salutes the great tradition of Crow bronc riders: "These are the men that know what it is like to become a part of the horse, to be in time and to know what the horse is going to do before he does it." One Lakota bronc rider read such a passage and informed bystanders that since a little rivalry still remains between the Lakotas and the Crows he would demonstrate to one and all where the truly great bronc riders live.

The national finals furnish comparable rivalries. Competitors will comment on how representatives of their regional association fare compared to representatives from another region. In 1986 the Canadians were delighted to note the accomplishments of Canadian cowboys and cowgirls, but disaster struck two years later when, for the first time in the history of the INFR, Canadians won no championships. The headline in *Windspeaker* groaned: "Canucks Bite the Dust at Albuquerque Rodeo." The primary emphasis, however, remains on tribe. Mike Bruised Head's story on the 1986 INFR for the *Kainai News* therefore is headlined: "Blood & Cheyenne Cowboys Dominate 11th Annual INFR." At the 1995 INFR, the Standing Rock Sioux Tribe sponsored an advertisement in the program. It read in part: "We at Standing Rock are especially proud that Terry Joe Fisher, a tribal member, is participating at this rodeo as a finalist. We join his parents in their support of him."

At the same time, Indian rodeo provides a place for Native peoples to reaffirm their identities as Indians. The Standing Rock advertisement goes on to say: "This is an event where we have the opportunity to come together as friends and enjoy watching our favorite riders compete." Tsuu T'ina barrel racer Sandra Crowchild comments: "I competed at pro rodeo but I felt like I was going to a job. At Indian rodeo there is bonding because we're all Indians." Fred Gladstone adds that when he and other Blood cowboys travel to distant locales, "other nations welcome us and wish us a safe journey."

At fourteen years of age,
Glenna Goodstoney rides
steers, but looks forward to
riding bulls. Indian Pro
Rodeo Association Finals,
Morley, Alberta, October
1996.

Competition and Achievement

Torrin Kaquitts races to distract the steer when a young rider dismounts at the Father's Day Rodeo, Morley, Alberta, June 1996.

Facing page: Airborne. Cowboy and bull part company at the Inter-Tribal Ceremonial Rodeo, Church Rock, New Mexico, August 1996.

Competition and Achievement

85

A bull rider at the Eastern
Navajo Fair and Rodeo in
Crownpoint, New Mexico,
July 1994.

Facing page: When cowboys
are hurt, paramedics and
ambulance are ready.
Ahoohai Days Rodeo,

Holbrook, Arizona, July
1994.

We see in such distinctions how Indian rodeo is both a product of Native engagement with other societies and an entity separate unto itself. Ultimately it is a synthesis of elements from elsewhere, including horses, cattle, the cowboy culture, and its organizational structure, combined with features that mark its ethnic boundaries. One is reminded of how African Americans responded to being rejected by White churches in the nineteenth century. They formed their own churches, such as the African Methodist Episcopal Church, which furnished outlets for leadership, provided opportunities for distinct cultural expressions (such as gospel singing), and reemphasized group identity. Indian rodeo, too, has encouraged leadership, offered the chance for powwows and giveaways, and clearly reinforced group ties. As in powwow dance competitions, you want to demonstrate your talent, be proud of who you are, and enjoy all that accompanies the scene. It is important to remember that in the North American West, there remains virulent prejudice against Indians. There continue to be roadblocks against many other forms of achievement. Rodeo offers the chance to demonstrate to yourself, your family, and your community that you can do something very well indeed. There is honor in the competition for all who reveal a degree of determination and skill. Thus you don't have to

finish first all the time to be deemed a success. In other sports, in team games like basketball, the line between winning (and success) and losing (and failure) seems more pronounced.

Indian rodeo thus makes us reevaluate what we mean by success. Some competitors win often; others rarely win. All pay the entry fee, conscious of the odds. In barrel racing and the roping events, competitors believe they have some control over how things will turn out, but even then their chances may be hamstrung by an injury, either to them or to their horse. A week before the INFR in Saskatoon, Sandra Crowchild broke three fingers while doctoring her horse, Big Man. She competed in spite of the pain, but her chance for victory had vanished. In the roughstock events, a rider may draw a horse that won't buck or a bull so full of himself that the cowboy swears no one, not even Jim Shoulders, could have stayed on him that day. You might blame a judge for not doing his job in evaluating your ride. The weather in Morley may be so miserable that entrants feel as if they deserve awards just for being there. Or, although they hate to admit it, there are occasions when they just flat out got beat. Someone else really had a great day. Before he departed for Saskatoon for the INFR in 1996, steer wrestler Richard Bish (Tsuu T'ina) smiled and said: "I didn't leave home for second." After he was edged out of winning the title by Howard Edmondson's great performance, he smiled again and acknowledged, "Well, it didn't work out, but second's better than third."

When we think about competition and achievement in the world of Indian rodeo, we need to see more than what occurs in the sudden burst of activity in the arena. Part of competing involves what you do beforehand and afterwards. A rodeo day proceeds in stages, each marked by predictable rituals and, upon occasion, some unwelcome surprises. According to an old saying, people do better in dealing with the unanticipated if they just have some advance warning. Yet life isn't always that accommodating. You don't count on the news that your grandmother has taken ill or your cousin has been in a serious accident.

You don't expect that the horse trailer will have a flat tire or your truck's engine will wheeze: "OK, that's it. I've been abused long enough. I've had it. I quit."

Competition means driving from one place to another to another to another, drinking bad coffee, and eating food your mind and body can't immediately forget. It means traveling with your dad or your mom or your spouse or your buddies, trying to find the right kind of music on the radio, trying to concentrate, trying to relax. You arrive at the arena at the last minute or too late and find yourself disqualified, or you arrive early and have time to kill. As you wait, you stretch, pace, joke, wonder about what the day will bring. After you have competed and your event has concluded, if your family is on hand, you look for them and prepare for congratulation or consolation. You know that if you've brought your two-year-old daughter along she will love you whatever the result. You look for her and you do your best to smile if it hasn't gone the way you had hoped. If the results are dismal, then there will be more time to ponder what to do next.

We all have different standards for success. In school, a B+ is failure for one student but equals climbing Mount Everest for another. What a former champion deems dismal might be an unprecedented achievement for someone else. Regardless of indi-

Steer wrestling is tough
enough on a dry day, without the benefit of mud. But
there's nothing you can do
about the weather. You just
compete. Dallas Young Pine
entered bull riding, saddle
bronc, and calf roping on
this day. Tsuu T'ina Nation
Rodeo, Alberta, July 1993.

vidual yardsticks, there comes a time when some cowboys and cowgirls do call a halt, temporarily or permanently, to this chapter in their lives. That decision, if it ever emerges, will be reached with the greatest reluctance. A more typical response is: I have worked too hard, I have invested too much time and money to quit now. Or this: I can't quit. I haven't realized my dreams or the dreams others have for me. Or this: I am just too stubborn, too knot-headed, too ornery to quit.

Success in the junior ranks may indicate future greatness, yet there are always those who start out well and—for various reasons—don't realize their potential. Others are late bloomers, who grow into the sport as they mature physically and socially. Still others eventually discover that they have more potential in one event than another. Kevin Littlelight (Tsuu T'ina) said that for a long time he wasn't good at anything except falling off horses. When he tried steer wrestling, "it just came naturally," and he finally relinquished his label as the "world's worst calf roper."

Wallace Stegner once labeled the American West "next year country." Competitors in Indian rodeo understand this sentiment. In rodeo you always look toward the next one, whether you've won or lost. When Andrew Hunt won the INFR all around, he said that his next ambition was to win a champi-

onship in one of the individual events. Three years later he achieved that objective, winning first place in bull riding. So if you win, you look to win again; if you haven't won, you look to win in the immediate future. The next rodeo will allow you to show that your win wasn't a fluke. The next rodeo will give you a chance to turn things around. You may be a young cowboy trying to get started or an older cowboy trying to keep going. You say: Wait till tomorrow. Wait till next week. Or, like a Chicago Cubs fan: Wait till next year.

It used to be that you fought and feared getting older. Today you may hope that somehow an exception to aging will be made in your case, but at least you can now look forward to continuing competition with your peers or even to resuming an activity that life had forced you to put aside. If at fifty you pose no threat to Jackson Sundown, you can still compete against other fifty-year-olds in special events designed for more senior participants. Whether labeled a senior, a master, an old-timer, a champion of yesterday, or a legend in your own mind, you probably welcome the chance to keep doing what you love. Even at sixty and seventy, you can smile, shake your head, and, depending on the occasion, say, "Thanks," or "Second is better than third," or "Better luck next time."

Bull rider Marshall Johnson
stops in the shade on a
90-degree afternoon at the
Inter-Tribal Ceremonial
Rodeo, Church Rock,
New Mexico, August 1996.

Injured in a recent rodeo,
senior bull riding champion
Wayne Yazzie attends the
Inter-Tribal Ceremonial
Rodeo, Church Rock,
New Mexico, August 1996,
to help his son in the bull
riding event.

Shawn Best demonstrated his versatility by qualifying in bull riding, saddle bronc, and bareback for the Indian National Finals Rodeo. This photograph was taken before his final bull ride. Saskatoon, Saskatchewan, November 1996.

Overleaf: A grandmother and her grandson, a true Indian cowboy, on a float in the Canada Day Parade, Canada Day Rodeo, Morley, Alberta, July 1997.

CHAPTER FIVE

Legacy

Chance Hall Buffalo (Cree) can't imagine a world without horses. His mother, Carolyn, is a barrel racer and breakaway roper. He has traveled with her to many different rodeos and has learned about some of the qualities prized in this environment. When he was two years old he accompanied his mother to the Buffalo Ranch Rodeo. Carolyn asked Linda MacCannell if she would take his photograph. Usually Linda would never photograph a child that young with a view camera. It takes too long to set up the shot. But Chance seemed patient, and Linda, a mother of three sons, was delighted with his appearance in his leather chaps, western shirt, and cowboy hat. All Carolyn had to say was: "Chance, stand there." He did.

As Linda continued over the next several years to photograph Native children at rodeos, she kept encountering that quality of patience. These children also tended to be calm, for they already understood the significance of concentration. They also reflected a pride in their own achievements and in the accomplishments of others. They knew they could not win without the help of family. Whether they were barrel racers or ropers, they also knew they could not win without a good horse. When Linda asked eight-year-old barrel racer Jenna Jake if she could take her photograph, Jenna agreed, on one condition. Her horse, Molly Duck, had to be in the picture.

Of course participation in rodeo is no panacea for individuals of any generation. Yet for the young people of many Native communities rodeo continues to provide an experience significant beyond wins and losses. I have suggested in these pages that this significance is tied to generations, to family, to community, and to heritage. Although athletes and writers often claim too much for what sports may teach, it seems apparent that this particular activity fosters characteristics that will prove useful in the new century, just as they have in the past. In interview after interview, in one published source after another, one hears this consistent refrain.

Perhaps some readers might think that such concerns are less relevant with the advent of casinos. They would be well advised, however, to disregard almost all they have read or heard on this subject. Although casinos have brought to some Indian nations unprecedented revenues, they have not presented the same profits to all Indian nations. One cannot know, even for the most profitable enterprises, how long they will yield such returns or what positive or negative long-term effects they will have. Some communities with the most deeply rooted problems are distant from large bases of pop-ulation and have not profited much from this new source of revenue. Alcoholism, severe unemployment, and diabetes persist in many places.

Regardless of their contemporary economic status, Indian children will come to maturity facing questions much like those that confronted their parents, grandparents, and great-grandparents. They will still have to make complex decisions about the direction of their lives as they assess the options available to themselves, their families, and their communities in the twenty-first century.

There is more reason for hope at the end of this century than when the 1800s concluded. Janine Pease Pretty on Top (Crow), president of Little Big Horn College, became a grandmother in the summer of 1997. Her new status gave her additional cause to weigh the "tenacious respect for life and homelands" that her grandparents had demonstrated. She believed that "future Native peoples will have the survivorship, the inventiveness, and the adaptive abilities of their parents and grandparents."

Janine Pease Pretty on Top would be the first to affirm that all Indian nations are less insular than they were even a decade ago. Television influences profoundly the worldview of today's children. Kids mimic Bart Simpson and Michael Jordan. An increasing number feel comfortable with computers, but

Barrel racer Jenna Jake, at eight years of age, is already a seasoned and highly successful barrel racer. She and her horse, Molly Duck, proved tough to beat. Eastern Navajo Fair and Rodeo, Crownpoint, New Mexico, July 1994.

Facing page: Chance Hall
Buffalo, two and a half
years of age, seems destined
for rodeo stardom. Buffalo
Ranch Rodeo, Hobbema,
Alberta, August 1993.

Steer rider Bryan Labelle
reflects pride and assurance.
Morley Rodeo, Alberta,
September 1993.

Desmond Lambert is ready
to follow in his father's
footsteps at the Kainai Fair
and Rodeo, Standoff,
Alberta, July 1993.

an increasing number in many communities also struggle with the influence of drugs and contribute to the escalating degree of violence. In Arizona, the tentacles of Tucson extend toward once isolated Indian communities. In Alberta, the Calgary metropolitan area begins to knock on the door of the Tsuu T'ina reserve. Such proximity creates new problems for that Native enclave. Bedford Littlelight spoke about the utility of his teen-aged sons' participating in rodeo "I know with the Sarcee, and other reserves, we are so close to cities that many of the boys are tempted to get involved with bad habits such as drugs and booze and then bring them back to the reserve." "If you give them something else to do," Littlelight noted, "then they realize there are better ways to enjoy life and what it has to give back to you."

Eugene Charley expressed similar sentiments. Nearly three decades ago, I watched him receive his diploma as one of the first graduates of Navajo Community College. Now, in January 1998, he spoke to participants in the Indian Junior Rodeo Association and articulated what he had demonstrated to me and other NCC faculty members many years ago: rodeo helps you believe in yourself, focus on the work at hand, and prepare for new challenges. He had realized in the late 1960s that if he could ride bulls, he certainly ought to be able to earn a university degree. After he graduated, he taught on the Navajo Nation and eventually became superintendent of the Kayenta school district. Along the way he initiated a bull riding school and founded the Indian Junior Rodeo Association.

On that January evening, Eugene Charley looked out on the overflow crowd at the Red Rock State Park auditorium. He saw hundreds of young cowboys and cowgirls receive recognition for their performance during the past rodeo season. Reporter Cate Gilles observed, "But no matter where they placed, the kids gave their parents a lot of reason to be proud of all their hard work and dedication. Every kid walking off the stage with an award also took an earsplitting grin back to the table to share with their mom and dad." Here, then, were "kids who have something to do and who carry on the rodeo traditions of pride and hard work." For Eugene Charley, the night offered the chance to preach his ABCs of life: "A stands for having a good attitude. B is to always, always believe in yourself and do the very best that you can. C is to concentrate and focus on the task at hand. And D is to stay away from drugs and alcohol and things that can really hurt you if you let them."

The IJRA division all around winners and the new IJRA queen had heeded the message. The *Navajo Times* featured a photograph of the six young people, all standing in front of their new saddles. Midget division champion Emerson Long Jr., of Twin Lakes, New Mexico, is not much bigger than his saddle. To his immediate right in the photograph is the all around champion of the peewee division, Jenna Jake.

In the eastern part of the Navajo Nation and elsewhere in the Indian West, a smaller percentage of the people now earn a living from the land. The workings of reservation economies have encouraged urbanization. A great many people have moved into town, closer to jobs and schools. Far fewer children today grow up like Bill Kine, in the midst of sheep herds. They are less likely to have the responsibility of herding sheep or rounding up cattle or taking on a variety of tasks inherent in rural life. For many Native young people, then, rodeo provides a kind of routine, an expectation of taking care of business, a predictable pattern. Many of their older relatives believe that this experience will serve them well when they later must assume adult responsibilities. The travel and the opportunities to meet other people and to experience other places will also assist the increasing percentage of Indian students who attend distant colleges and universities.

At those schools, they will likely fare better because they understand the nature of competition. Competition within the world of Indian rodeo has become more rigorous with each passing year. Cowboys and cowgirls will have their performances videotaped so they can observe errors and correct them. They will enroll in special schools designed to improve their results in a particular event. They will practice more hours. They will attempt to ride more demanding broncs and bulls. They will demand as much or more of themselves than their predecessors of earlier generations. They will know that the margin of victory is almost always slim.

Marvin Redhorse said, "I consider myself an athlete. . . . I'm a competitor. I think you've got to stay physically fit. . . . You've got to get up every morning and think about it seriously. The animals out here—they don't have any sympathy on you." He concluded, "I always wanted to make time for rodeo. It was like a dream for me. My dad's done it, so I'm a second-generation cowboy. I tell myself to never quit and just try hard, try hard."

Barrel racer Laverne Gene (Navajo) agreed. "I guess it is like any sport, the more you practice, the more you work on the details. In the beginning, I felt like I was just donating my money to the winners. Once you place, though, the competitive juices flow and you want to practice harder."

Most young rodeo contestants will also build from the foundation of family, of which rodeo has been an

A young cowboy enjoys his
prominence on the hood of
a truck on the Canada Day

Parade, Canada Day
Rodeo, Morley, Alberta,
July 1997.

Legacy

103

Facing page: Any young cowpoke appreciates a helping hand. Beaver Memorial Rodeo, near Morley, Alberta, June 1995.

Spectators hold their breath as a little mutton buster rockets out of the chutes at the Canada Day Rodeo, Morley, Alberta, June 1997.

Benjamin Cleveland, steer
rider, ponders his prospects.
He won the event that
afternoon at the A Bar C
Bull Riders Classic in Fort
Defiance, Arizona,
September 1993.

Keisha Barton knows she
soon will be a barrel racer.
Inter-Tribal Ceremonial
Rodeo, Church Rock,
New Mexico, August 1994.

integral part. Rodeo continues to encourage members of different generations to spend time together in shared interests. It even inspires younger people to think that older people still have something valuable to teach them. It presents a means through which an individual can recognize and respect the talents and achievements of people, both older and younger.

Unlike one hundred years ago, the conventional wisdom no longer holds that Indians are going to disappear. However, we still hear about the likelihood of other forms of disappearance. Observers predict that some languages will no longer be spoken, that certain ceremonies will no longer be conducted, that other specific components of Native life will wither and die. Such doomsayers are countered by many others who concur with Janine Pease Pretty on Top: "The new generations will take the Native life path with less burden, and build new traditions that protect the homelands, the culture and traditions, and carry the language into another millennium."

Ultimately the form and the appearance of Native societies matter less than their substance, their core, their heart. D'Arcy McNickle, the man of Cree descent who had been enrolled on the Flathead reservation, always underscored this point. In *Native American Tribalism: Indian Survivals and Renewals*, he emphasized: "The Indians, for all that

has been lost or rendered useless out of their ancient experience, remain a continuing ethnic and cultural enclave with a stake in the future." They had succeeded in this regard, McNickle argued, because they knew how to create boundaries that reinforced identity; they knew how to forge institutions that worked and that reminded the people who they were. Rodeo has been one of those institutions. It furnishes one clear example that the underlying values and priorities of Indian life will endure.

When Luci Tapahonso pictured her granddaughter's birth, she wrote of Chamisa Bah arriving "amid a herd of horses." The yellow and blue and white and black horses of the four directions were a part of Chamisa Bah's beginnings. "You will," Tapahonso affirmed, "grow strong like the horses of your past. You will grow strong like the horses of your birth."

At the birth of a new century, rodeo is an integral part of the Indian past, present, and future. It is an ongoing tradition. It is a legacy. It is one of the reasons why the next generation will grow strong. It begins with horses.

After a long day, family
members provide the best
welcome. Many Fingers

Lazy-B Memorial Rodeo,
near Standoff, Alberta, June
1997.

GLOSSARY

RODEO TERMS AND EVENTS

All around: Award for best overall performance in a particular rodeo or for the rodeo season.

Bareback bronc riding: One of the roughstock events; the rider, without a rein, saddle, or stirrups, but aided by a hand-hold built into the rigging, tries to stay on the horse for eight seconds.

Barrel racing: A timed event in which the rider completes a cloverleaf pattern around three barrels in the arena and then returns to her starting point. For each barrel that is knocked over there is a penalty of added time.

Breakaway roping: A timed event in which the rider's rope is attached by a string to the saddle horn; after the rope is thrown over the calf's head, the rider lets go of it. Timing ends after the calf pulls the string off the saddle horn.

Bronc (bronco): A horse, willing to buck, used in the bareback and saddle events.

Bulldogging: See Steer wrestling.

Bull riding: One of the roughstock events, in which the cowboy attempts to stay on the bull for eight seconds.

Calf roping: A timed event in which one person on horseback chases after a calf and attempts to throw a rope over its head. If that attempt succeeds, the cowboy/cowgirl dismounts, runs over to the calf, throws it down, and wraps three of its legs together with a second rope.

Chute: An enclosure that holds livestock.

Circuit: A series of rodeos over the course of a season to which one travels in order to compete.

Dally: After the animal is caught, the roper makes several wraps, or dallies, of the rope around the saddle horn.

Flag racing: A timed event in which the rider carries a flag from one part of the arena to another, where a second flag has been placed in a bucket of oats on top of a barrel. The cowboy/cowgirl takes the flag from the bucket, then rides to a second barrel and takes that flag from the bucket, and returns to the starting point.

Goat tying: A timed event in which the contestant rides to a point in the arena, dismounts, and ties (in the manner of calf roping) three of the legs of a goat. The goat is tied to a stake with a rope, generally about 15 feet in length. In goat tail tying, the contestant ties a ribbon to the goat's tail.

Hazer: In the steer wrestling event, a second rider who rides alongside the steer and keeps it running in a straight line.

Header: One of the two participants in team roping, with the responsibility for roping the steer's head, dallying his rope, and getting out of the way of the heeler, who attempts to catch (throw a rope around) the steer's heels.

Heeler: The other participant in team roping, who after catching the steer's heels, must dally his rope, and then face the header.

Loop: The noose in the catch rope.

Mutton bustin': An event in which the contestant is put on a sheep inside a small chute. After the chute gate is opened he/she attempts to ride the sheep across the arena.

Pole bending: A timed event in which the contestant rides in a slalom pattern through a course of six poles placed about 20 feet apart and then returns to the starting line. There is a penalty of added time for each pole knocked over.

Ribbon roping: An event in which the rider ropes a calf and then a runner runs to the calf, takes a ribbon that has been tied to its tail, and runs to the finish line.

Roughstock: Events in which cowboys try to ride broncs or bulls.

Saddle bronc riding: One of the roughstock events, in which the entrant rides a bronc with a saddle. Today the competitor tries to continue for eight seconds, but in early rodeo the bronc had to be ridden to a standstill.

Steer decorating: A timed event in which the competitor does not bulldog a steer but decorates it by placing an elastic band with a red ribbon over its horns.

Steer undecorating: A timed event in which the entrant rides to a steer and undecorates it by taking off a ribbon that has been attached to its back.

Steer riding: One of the roughstock events for younger contestants, in which the rider attempts to stay on the steer for eight seconds.

Steer wrestling: A timed event in which, aided by the hazer, the steer wrestler (dogger) rides up to a steer running across the arena, drops onto the steer's head and shoulder, grabs its horns, and throws it to the ground.

Team roping: A timed event involving two ropers, in which the header ropes the head of the steer and the heeler then ropes the steer's hind legs and turns his/her horse to face the steer and the header.

Timed events: Such events as barrel racing, calf roping, steer wrestling, and team roping.

Wild cow milking: A rodeo event in which a rider ropes a range (or wild) cow and a second cowboy (the mugger) holds the cow, milks her, and then takes that small amount of milk in a container and runs to the finish line.

INDIAN COMMUNITIES

This list includes the names of Indian peoples mentioned in the book. "Reservation" is a term employed in the United States;

"reserve" is the comparable term in Canada. Both refer to land that is held in trust status, or reserved, for the particular group. It is used here without positive or negative connotation. Oklahoma (other than the underground oil resources of the Osages) does not have reservation land but does, of course, include many Indian communities. In many, but not all instances today the specific reservation/reserve/community refers to itself as a nation. "Tribe" is another term employed, although less universally than in the past. In their own languages, many nations or tribes refer to themselves as "the people." A band is a smaller group of people that united to search for food and became, over time, a social unit.

The terms "Indian" and "Native" are employed in this book. There is no one term that all people accept. Many individuals prefer to be known as "Indians," but "Native" (rather than "Native American") is now also often used. In Canada "First Nations" and "Aboriginal" are used, but these terms have not been frequently adopted in the United States.

Apache: People of the U.S. Southwest, with two reservations today in Arizona, two reservations in New Mexico, and two communities in Oklahoma.

Blackfeet (Blackfoot): People of the northern Plains. Term describes the Blackfoot reserve in Alberta, the Blackfeet reservation in Montana, and the confederacy of related communities: Blackfeet, Blood, and Peigan.

Blood: Part of the Blackfeet confederacy; reserve in Alberta.

Cherokee: The western Cherokee today reside in eastern Oklahoma.

Cheyenne: People of the Plains, divided today into the Northern Cheyenne reservation in Montana and the Southern Cheyenne community in Oklahoma.

Comanche: People of the southern Plains; community today in Oklahoma.

Confederated Salish and Kootenai: Affiliated groups who today occupy the Flathead reservation in Montana.

Cree: People primarily residing in Canada, from the Rocky Mountain and Plains country east to Hudson's Bay. There are ten Plains Cree reserves in southern and central Alberta. Sometimes linked to Chippewa (Ojibwe) groups, including the Chippewa-Cree community on the Rocky Boy reservation in Montana.

Crow: People of the Plains, residing today on the Crow reservation in southeastern Montana.

Flathead: Reservation name for the Confederated Salish and Kootenai community of Montana.

Fort Berthold: Reservation name for the Three Affiliated Tribes community of North Dakota.

Gros Ventre: People of the northern Plains, residing today on the Fort Belknap reservation in northern Montana.

Hopi: Pueblo Indian people whose reservation is in northern Arizona.

Jicarilla Apache: Apache people whose reservation is in northern New Mexico.

Kiowa: People of the southern Plains; community today in Oklahoma.

Lakota (Western or Teton Sioux): Divided into seven bands, this is the largest Native group of the northern Plains; in addition to a small population in Canada, most primarily reside today in South Dakota, with the Standing Rock reservation including land in both North and South Dakota.

Modoc: The people reside primarily today in the California-Oregon border area and in Oklahoma.

Muscogee (Creek): People originally from the southeastern United States, who reside today primarily in eastern Oklahoma.

Nakoda (Stoney): People of the northern Plains, who live today on five reserves in Alberta; in Montana, the term employed is Assiniboine (who share the Fort Belknap and Fort Peck reservations).

Navajo (Diné): A people of the U.S. Southwest who are linguistically related to the Apaches; the Navajo Nation is the largest reservation in the United States, covering about 25,000 square miles in Arizona, New Mexico, and Utah.

Nez Perce: People of the Plateau region who reside primarily on the Nez Perce reservation in Idaho but also on the Colville reservation in eastern Washington.

Oglala: One of the seven bands of the Lakotas; most Oglalas live on the Pine Ridge reservation in western South Dakota.

Pawnee: A central Plains people who reside primarily today in eastern Oklahoma, but historically are centered in Nebraska.

Peigan: Part of the Blackfeet Confederacy; reserve in Alberta.

Pine Ridge: Lakota reservation in western South Dakota.

Rosebud: Lakota reservation in western South Dakota.

Standing Rock: Lakota reservation with acreage in both North Dakota and South Dakota.

Three Affiliated Tribes (Arikara, Hidatsa, and Mandan): People of the northern Plains who reside today on the Fort Berthold reservation in North Dakota.

Tohono O'odham (Papago): People of the Sonoma desert whose reservations are in southern Arizona.

Tsuu T'ina (Sarcee): People of the northern Plains whose reserve is in Alberta, near Calgary.

Yakama: People of the Plateau region whose reservation is in central Washington.

SOURCES   CHAPTER ONE: HISTORY

LaVerne Harrell Clark, *They Sang for Horses: The Impact of the Horse on Navajo and Apache Folklore* (Tucson: University of Arizona Press, 1966), and Aileen O'Bryan, *The Diné: Origin Myths of the Navaho Indians* (Washington, D.C.: Smithsonian Institution, Bureau of American Ethnology Bulletin 163, 1956), provided the initial quotations and general information about Navajos and their horses. "The Horse," a 1997–99 exhibit at the Heard Museum in Phoenix, Arizona, furnished information about tribal names and the importance of horses to different Native communities. Joseph Medicine Crow, *From the Heart of the Crow Country: The Crow Indians' Own Stories* (New York: Orion Books, 1992), yielded perceptions about the Crows and horses; the quotation by Joseph Medicine Crow is from this book. The general consideration of Indian cattle ranching is derived from Peter Iverson, *When Indians Became Cowboys: Native Peoples and Cattle Ranching in the American West* (Norman: University of Oklahoma Press, 1994). The discussion of assimilation is drawn from Peter Iverson, *"We Are Still Here": American Indians in the Twentieth Century* (Wheeling, Ill.: Harlan Davidson, 1998). Wayne S. Wooden and Gavin Ehringer, *Rodeo in America: Wranglers, Roughstock, and Paydirt* (Lawrence: University Press of Kansas, 1996), and Kristine Fredriksson, *American Rodeo: From Buffalo Bill to Big Business* (College Station: Texas A&M University Press, 1985), offered information about the start and evolution of rodeo. Consideration of Indian participation in Wild West shows is based upon L. G. Moses, *Wild West Shows and the Images of American Indians, 1883–1933* (Albuquerque: University of New Mexico Press, 1996), and Edward L. Renno, "The Wild and Wonderful Magic of the 101 Ranch," *Persimmon Hill* 12, no. 3 (1982): 8–21. The status of women in rodeo is analyzed by Mary Lou LeCompte, *Cowgirls of the Rodeo: Pioneer Professional Athletes* (Urbana: University of Illinois Press, 1993). The works cited above by Wooden and Ehringer, Fredriksson, amd LeCompte, as well as Fred Schnell, *Rodeo!: The Suicide Circuit* (Chicago: Rand McNally, 1971), are sources of information about contemporary rodeo events. The material about Tom Three Persons is based on a discussion with Hugh Dempsey in June 1997 and on Hugh A. Dempsey, *Tom Three Persons: Legend of an Indian Cowboy* (Saskatoon: Purich Publishing, 1997). Caen Bly, "History of the IRCA," Kainawa Rodeo program, July 15–18, 1993, and Glen Mikkelson, "Indians and Rodeo," *Alberta History* 35, no. 3 (Summer 1987): 13–19, and an extended interview with Fred Gladstone in June 1997 provided details about the achievements of Canadian rodeo cowboys. Crow Nation Fair and Rodeo programs told about the evolution of Crow Fair and Rodeo. The July 4th celebration on Rosebud is depicted in *The Sioux of the Rosebud: A History in Pictures* (Norman: University of Oklahoma Press, 1971), with text by Henry W. Hamilton and Jean Tyree Hamilton and photographs by John A. Anderson. The description of the Tohono O'odham Fair and Rodeo is drawn from "Papagos Manage Their Own Fair and Rodeo," *Indians at Work* (Washington, D.C.: Bureau of Indian Affairs, March, 1939), 19–20. The quotation from Bronco Martinez is from "Navajo Rodeo Cowboys," produced by KNME of Albuquerque, New Mexico. The discussion of the evolution of regional associations and the Indian National Finals Rodeo is derived from the interview with Fred Gladstone, the conversation with Hugh Dempsey, Indian National Finals Rodeo programs, various stories about Indian rodeo in Canadian Native newspapers such as the *Kainai News* and *Windspeaker*, and articles by Oree Foster in the *Navajo Times*, including "AIRCA Celebrating 37 Years," January 27, 1994;

"AIRCA Heading Into 37th Year of Rodeo," April 21, 1994; "1994 INFR Moving to Rapid City, S.D.," February 3, 1994; "AIPRCA World Finals Is Here," September 26, 1996; "Begay Wins All-Around," October 3, 1996; "AIPRCA Hosting 2nd World Finals at Red Rock," September 25, 1997; and "Begay Is Big Winner at AIPRCA 1997 World Finals Rodeo," October 2, 1997.

CHAPTER TWO: PLACE

The quotation from Joy Harjo is from her *Secrets from the Center of the World* (Tucson: University of Arizona Press, 1989). Monty Roessel's observations are included in his article "Ride 'em Cowgirl," *New Mexico Magazine*, August 1997, 60–67. Klara Bonsack Kelley and Harris Francis, *Navajo Sacred Places* (Bloomington: Indiana University Press, 1994), and Keith H. Basso, *Wisdom Sits in Places: Landscape and Language Among the Western Apache* (Albuquerque: University of New Mexico Press, 1996), offer valuable perceptions about the people and the land. The discussion of the powwow is informed by Charlotte Heth, ed., *Native American Dance: Ceremonies and Social Traditions* (Washington, D.C.: Smithsonian Institution, 1992); Elizabeth S. Grobsmith, *Lakota of the Rosebud: A Contemporary Ethnography* (New York: Holt, Rinehart, & Winston, 1981), provided information about powwows and giveaways. For the parade as a metaphor for the Crow experience, see Frederick E. Hoxie, *Parading Through History: The Making of the Crow Nation in America, 1805–1935* (New York: Cambridge University Press, 1995). Conversations with Fred Gladstone, Hugh Dempsey, and Floyd Many Fingers at the Many Fingers Rodeo helped shape my depiction of that rodeo. Also helpful was Caen Bly, "History of the IRCA," included in the Kainawa Rodeo program, July 15–18, 1993. A conversation with Jess Beaver in Morley and the program for the Canada Day Rodeo in Morley furnished information about this event. Conversations with Myla Vicenti Carpio and Thurza Vicenti centrally influenced my depiction of the Little Beaver Rodeo. Information about the chicken pull is contained in "Chicken Pull," *Diné Baa-Hani*, March 1, 1973, and "The First Ramah Rodeos," *Tsa' Adzi*', Ramah Navajo School Board, 1973. The advertisement for the Playboys appeared in *Diné Baa-Hani*, January 1971. Conversations with Bill Kine and other individuals contributed to the description of the Eastern Navajo Fair and Rodeo. Information about the cultural importance of Mount Taylor and the surrounding area is contained in Ethelou Yazzie, ed., *Navajo History* (Rough Rock, Ariz.: Navajo Curriculum Center, Rough Rock Demonstration School, 1971), and in Luci Tapahonso, "This Is How They Were Placed for Us," in Tapahonso, *Blue Horses Rush In: Poems and Stories* (Tucson: University of Arizona Press, 1997), 39–42.

CHAPTER THREE: FAMILY AND TRADITION
The quotations from Gabriel Begaye and Jack Jackson are from Gabriel Begaye, "The Indian Cowboy and Cowgirl in Indian and Professional Rodeo," a paper completed for a class I taught at Arizona State University. The material on the Gladstone family is based primarily upon the interview conducted with Fred Gladstone in June 1997. Gladstone family history is also included in Flora Zaharia and Leo Fox, *Kitomahkitapiiminnoooniksi: Stories from Our Elders* (Edmonton: Kainawa Board of Education, 1995), vol. 2. Charles Ursenbach's interview of Fred Gladstone took place on June 4, 1975, and is included in the Charles Ursenbach oral history collection at the Glenbow Museum in Calgary. The letter from Fred Gladstone to his parents is in the Gladstone family materials at the Glenbow. Robbie Whitchair is quoted in the *Navajo Times*, March 28, 1991. The *Navajo Times* also furnished

information about the Diné Land Senior Rodeo Association. The material about Jess Beaver is drawn from a conversation in June 1997 and an article in *Rodeo Times*, June 1993. The material on Pat Provost is contained in a brochure for "The Canadian Cowboy" exhibit at the Glenbow Museum in the summer of 1997. The discussion of the Bruised Heads and the Indian Rodeo Cowboys Association is based on Caen Bly, "History of the IRCA," Kainawa Rodeo program, July 15–18, 1993, and Glen Mikkelson, "Indians and Rodeo," *Alberta History* 35, no. 3 (Summer 1987): 13–19. The quotation from Carole Jackson is included in the KNME video on Navajo rodeo. Dennis Clah's characterization of Dean Jackson appeared in the 1993 Gallup Ceremonial program. Terry Lusty, "Ropin's a Real Family Affair," *Windspeaker*, June 17, 1988, provided information about the Yellowbirds. Jaymon J. Yazzie, "Ramone Brothers Are Top Team Ropers," *Navajo Times*, June 16, 1994, is the source for this subject. Bobby Benally's comments appeared in Susanne Anderson, *Song of the Earth Spirit* (New York: McGraw-Hill, 1973). Sonlatsa Jim-James's observation about her father is in Joy Harjo and Gloria Bird, eds., *Reinventing the Enemy's Language: Contemporary Native Women's Writing of North America* (New York: W. W. Norton, 1997). The tribute to Hobert Pourier is in Avis Little Eagle, "Hobert Pourier: A Legendary Cowboy Memorialized," *Indian Country Today*, February 18, 1993. The consideration of Crow rodeo is based on the Crow Fair and Rodeo program of 1994. Levi Black Water is remembered in Tom Russell, "One of Rodeo's Best," *Windspeaker*, May 24, 1991; an obituary published in the *Lethbridge Herald*, April 25, 1991; and programs for the Levi Black Water Memorial Rodeo. The tribute to Trevor "Tuffy" Holloway was published in the Kananaskis Rodeo program, July 21, 1996. The obituary for Dale David "Tazz" Big Plume was printed in the *Calgary Herald*, February 10, 1994. Joy Harjo, "The Place of Origins," is included in Lucy R. Lippard, ed., *Partial Recall* (New York: New Press, 1992).

CHAPTER FOUR: COMPETITION
AND ACHIEVEMENT

"The Bull Rider" was published in *Diné Baa-Hani*, January 1971. Elements of the heroic journey are discussed by Katherine Spencer, *Mythology and Values: An Analysis of Navaho Chantway Myths* (Philadelphia: American Folklore Society, 1957). The list of champions is included in programs from the Indian National Finals Rodeo. The quotation from Carole Jackson is from the video on Navajo rodeo produced by KNME of Albuquerque, New Mexico. Andrew Hunt is quoted in *Kainai News*, December 3, 1986; Lewis Little Bear's advertisement is printed in this same issue. Information about Native performances in the Calgary Stampede is included in Glen Mikkelson, "Indians and Rodeo," *Alberta History* 35, no. 3 (Summer 1987): 13–19, and Caen Bly, "History of the IRCA," Kainawa Rodeo program, July 15–18, 1993. "Indian Athletes Play for Lakota Nation, Oglala Band and Families" provides a profile of Dave Archambault; it is one of the essays included in Tim Giago, *News from Indian Country* (Pierre, S.D.: State Publishing Company, 1984), 132–36. Loretta Fowler discusses prominence and competition in *Shared Symbols, Contested Meanings: Gros Ventre Culture and History, 1778–1984* (Ithaca: Cornell University Press, 1987). Kevin Little-light is quoted in an article in *Windspeaker*, June 1996. The quotation about Crow riders is from the 1982 Crow Fair rodeo program. The Lakota bronc rider mentioned is Howard Hunter, depicted by Joan Morrison in "Indian Rodeo," *Native Peoples* 2, no. 4 (Summer 1989): 22–23. "Canucks Bite the Dust at Albuquerque Rodeo" was published in *Windspeaker*, December 2, 1988. Sandra Crowchild is interviewed by Doug Cut Hand in a Canadian Broadcasting Company video. Fred Gladstone showed this video to us in June 1997. Fred Gladstone's comments about competition also inform this discussion. Wallace Stegner discussed the West as next year country in "Finding the Place: A Migrant Childhood," included in his collection of essays *When the Bluebird Sings to the Lemonade Springs* (New York: Random House, 1992), 3–21.

CHAPTER FIVE: LEGACY

Janine Pease Pretty on Top's "Viewpoint" appeared in *Native Peoples* 11, no. 1 (Fall 1997): 44. The quotation from Bedford Littlelight is in Scott Ross, "Rodeo Veteran Littlelight Shows the Way," *Kainai News*, July 19, 1990. Eugene Charley and young cowboys and cowgirls are profiled by Cate Gilles, "IJRA Honors Young Cowboys, Cowgirls," *Navajo Times*, January 29, 1998. Marvin Redhorse's comments are in the KNME video on Navajo rodeo. Laverne Gene is quoted in Monty Roessel, "Ride 'em Cowgirl," *New Mexico Magazine*, August 1997. A book for children by Diane Hoyt-Goldsmith, *Apache Rodeo* (New York: Holiday House, 1995), emphasizes the importance of family. D'Arcy McNickle, *Native American Tribalism: Indian Survivals and Renewals* (New York: Oxford University Press, 1973), 14–15, discusses Native continuity and change. "Blue Horses Rush In," a poem by Luci Tapahonso, yielded the title for her *Blue Horses Rush In: Poems and Stories* (Tucson: University of Arizona Press, 1997), 103–4.

INDEX

Index